Voting
for Peace

BROOKINGS STUDIES IN FOREIGN POLICY

The Brookings Institution is a private nonprofit organization devoted to research, education, and publication on important issues of domestic and foreign policy. Its principal purpose is to bring knowledge to bear on the major policy problems facing the American people.

On occasion Brookings authors produce relatively short studies that warrant immediate and broad circulation as contributions to public understanding of issues of current national importance. The Brookings Studies in Foreign Policy series is intended to make such studies available to a broad, general audience. In keeping with their purpose, these studies are not subjected to all of the formal review and verification procedures established for the Institution's research publications. As in all Brookings publications, the judgments, conclusions, and recommendations presented in the studies are solely those of the authors and should not be attributed to the trustees, officers, or other staff members of the Institution.

OTHER TITLES IN THE SERIES

How to Be a Cheap Hawk: The 1999 and 2000 Defense Budgets
   by Michael O'Hanlon

Saving Lives with Force: Military Criteria for Humanitarian Intervention
   by Michael O'Hanlon

Studies in Foreign Policy

Voting for Peace

Postconflict Elections in Liberia

TERRENCE LYONS

BROOKINGS INSTITUTION PRESS
Washington, D.C.

BMV 7320 -6/1

Copyright © 1999

THE BROOKINGS INSTITUTION
1775 Massachusetts Avenue, N.W., Washington, D.C. 20036

Library of Congress Cataloging-in-Publication data

Lyons, Terrence.
    Voting for peace : post-conflict elections in Liberia /
Terrence Lyons.
      p. cm.
   Includes bibliographical references and index.
   ISBN 0-8157-5353-5 (pbk. : alk. paper)
   1. Elections—Liberia. 2. Presidents—Liberia—Election—1997.
3. Liberia—History—Civil War, 1989—Peace. 4. Liberia—Politics
and government—1980- I. Title.
   JQ3929.A5 L96 1999
   324.96662'03—dc21   99-40205
                                                                  CIP

                     9 8 7 6 5 4 3 2 1

The paper used in this publication meets the minimum requirements
of the American National Standard for Information Sciences—
Permanence of Paper for Printed Library Materials, ANSI Z39.48-1984.

Typeset in Hiroshige and Copperplate

Composition by Harlowe Typography
Cottage City, Maryland

Printed by R. R. Donnelley and Sons
Harrisonburg, Virginia

FOREWORD

The international community has struggled in recent years to help war-torn countries end internal conflicts and bring to power new regimes that can sustain the peace. Elections have been increasingly incorporated in peace agreements as the instrument to end the war and legitimize a new government. In the 1990s, Cambodia, El Salvador, Angola, Mozambique, Bosnia, and Liberia have held postconflict elections. Such elections have a number of goals, most notably war termination and promoting democratization. Nevertheless, the outcomes have often been mixed. The 1997 election in Liberia, the focus of this book, illustrates the relationship between these twin objectives. It also demonstrates the need to recognize that, in some circumstances, quick and imperfect or even flawed elections that promote war termination but do little to advance democratization may be necessary in order to prevent a return to conflict. Understanding the Liberian elections is important not only for their implications for peace and democracy in that war-torn part of West Africa but also for the lessons they hold for other postconflict situations.

This volume by Terrence Lyons is the product of both scholarly research and direct involvement in the Liberian transition. Lyons, currently a research fellow at the International Peace Research Institute in

Oslo, Norway, wrote this manuscript while a fellow in the Foreign Policy Studies program of the Brookings Institution. He has written on both conflict resolution and democratization in Africa. Most recently he co-edited *African Reckoning: A Quest for Good Governance* with Francis Deng (Brookings, 1998). Between March and August 1997 he served as senior program adviser to The Carter Center's Election Mission in Monrovia, Liberia. In this capacity, he held discussions with all the major political leaders, civic organizations, the diplomatic community, and officials of the United Nations, the Economic Community of West African States, and international nongovernmental organizations.

The author wishes to thank his colleagues at The Carter Center for their support and ideas, especially President Jimmy Carter, Ambassador Gordon Streeb, Susan Palmer, Sara Tindall, Rob Black, and Kendall Dwyer. He also is in debt to his colleagues at the International Foundation for Elections Systems, in particular Denise Dauphinais. A number of individuals read and commented on the manuscript. In particular the author would like to thank Richard Haass, director of Foreign Policy Studies at the Brookings Institution, Stephen Stedman, Thomas Carothers, Agnieszka Paczynska, David Carroll, Tom Ofcansky, and Allison Boyer. All errors, of course, remain the author's.

This publication was made possible in part by financing from the U.S. Agency for International Development through the International Foundation for Elections Systems and The Carter Center. Brookings gratefully acknowledges this support.

The manuscript was edited by Theresa Walker, with staff assistance by Melissa Martinelli. Mary Mortensen prepared the index.

The views expressed in this book are those of the author and should not be ascribed to the people whose assistance is acknowledged above, to the organizations that supported the project, or to the trustees, officers, or staff members of the Brookings Institution.

MICHAEL H. ARMACOST
President

October 1998
Washington, D.C.

CONTENTS

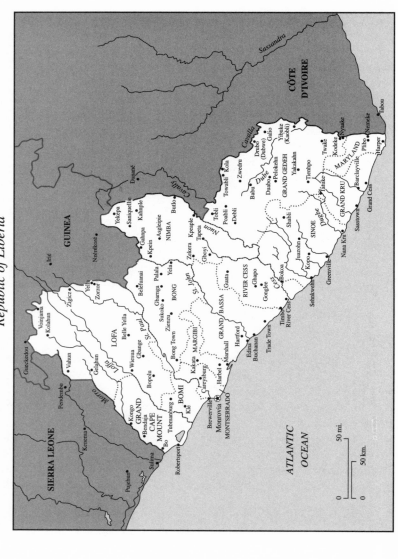

Republic of Liberia

1

ELECTIONS TO IMPLEMENT PEACE AGREEMENTS

A major challenge to international policy in recent years has been to find effective ways to assist war-torn societies to implement peace agreements and begin the process of rebuilding sustainable political, economic, and social institutions. The causes of internal conflicts are predominantly political; therefore the most critical element in rebuilding postconflict societies and preventing renewed conflict is an effective strategy for political reconstruction. In a range of cases, including Cambodia, El Salvador, Angola, Mozambique, Bosnia, and most recently Liberia, elections supported by the international community have been used to culminate transitional periods following internal conflict. Such postconflict elections are designed to serve as a strategy both to end a war and to initiate a process of democratization. The outcomes of these dual transitions to peace and democracy have been mixed, and the most important lessons for the international community have not been recognized. This study outlines patterns from recent transitions involving postconflict elections and then analyzes in greater detail the Liberian transition and the July 1997 elections in order to better understand the relationships between a peace process and the twin goals of war termination and transition to democracy.

On July 19, 1997, the Liberian people turned out in large numbers and voted overwhelmingly for former factional leader Charles Ghankay Taylor to be their president. Voting was peaceful, orderly, and watched by a large number of domestic and international observers and party poll watchers. The elections represented the final step in the implementation of the 1996 Abuja peace accords, the culmination of a series of thirteen peace agreements and a seven-year struggle to end civil violence.

The Liberian transition demonstrates both the potential and the limits of postconflict elections as a mechanism to facilitate conflict management and democratization. Comparative examination of other postconflict elections suggests that these dual goals are most likely to be met if the transitional process established in the peace agreement provides sufficient time and appropriate institutions to encourage security and the creation of peacetime political and civil structures before the voting.[1] The nature of the Liberian conflict and the Abuja peace process, however, required quick elections in an atmosphere in which leaders continued to derive power from their control over fighters and the structures of war remained effectively in place. Under these circumstances, the "least bad" policy outcome was to have an election that served important goals for ending the war but made less progress in promoting democratization.

The Liberian transitional process highlighted the relative strengths and weaknesses of the contending actors and the limited but nonetheless important opportunities for a new political order created by the Abuja peace process and regional peacekeeping. The elections marked a significant turning point in the conflict by providing a mechanism to permit Taylor and his supporters to ratify their claims to national authority. Voting reflected the political topography of Liberia after the distortions of seven years of war and allowed formal political authority and leadership to shift into greater congruence with actual power relationships. Given the nature of the Liberian conflict and the Abuja peace process, the ability to initiate a process of democratization simultaneously with ending the war was limited. Uneven access to resources and fear of renewed conflict shaped voting behavior, thus making the election more a referendum on peace than a democratic choice between meaningful options. Whether the election put in place leaders and institutions capable of sustaining the peace and promoting democratization in the longer term remains an open question with substantial reason for concern.

While elections inherently and appropriately should be associated with democratization, they also may serve other important roles. The international community should not cynically accept meaningless "demonstration elections" that legitimize authoritarian regimes without providing real scope for voter choice.[2] But neither should it insist that democratization is the only criteria by which to judge the value of postconflict elections.Other goals are also important, most notably war termination and allowing international patrons to disengage from troublesome clients. Which of the multiple goals tied to postconflict elections is most realized depends on the nature of the conflict, the peace agreement, and the interim government and on the ability of the international community to assist implementation of the agreement. The opportunity for a given election to serve as a tool of war termination may be greater than its potential for democratization.

In addition, the value of a postconflict election should be judged relative to the most likely alternatives available. If the transitional period can be prolonged to provide the time, space, and security for civil society and political parties to organize, then the dual goals of war termination and democratization are more likely to be met. If, however, postponing an election until democratization is more likely risks derailing the peace process and returning the country to war, it may be necessary to hold the election, implement the peace agreement, and focus on the postconflict government to promote democratization. Finally, if holding quick but flawed elections is more likely to ignite a new round of conflict that results in neither war termination nor democratization, then supporting the election is clearly dangerous and counterproductive. Judging whether supporting a postconflict election in a specific transition is more likely to promote both, one, or neither of the twin goals of war termination and democratization requires careful analysis and is inevitably easier to judge in hindsight. That, however, is inherently the nature of the policy challenges facing the international community in trying to assist peace building following civil war.

ELECTIONS, WAR TERMINATION, AND DEMOCRATIZATION

The outcomes of transitional periods after peace agreements that halt internal conflicts are critical to building a stable global order. The often brief time between cease-fire and elections is marked by multiple and difficult transitions. It is during these interims that war-torn societies struggle to construct legitimate political institutions, demobilize soldiers and resettle displaced populations, come to terms with past human rights abuses and begin to institutionalize rule of law, and initiate the process of moving economies from relief to development. They are periods of particular opportunity and risk as local leaders assess the relative benefits of working to sustain peace and build democracy in societies still polarized and distorted by war, where demagogues and spoilers can capitalize on people's fears. As a result, relatively small actions by the international community during these windows of opportunity often play a particularly important role in encouraging more responsible behavior and reducing the chances of backsliding into conflict and collapse. In particular, international attitudes toward and support of elections as a strategy to implement the peace accords and create new political institutions have been important in shaping the outcomes.

An examination of recent cases suggests that elections sometimes have succeeded in providing a mechanism for selecting new political leadership and institutions capable of preserving the peace. This seems to be the result in El Salvador, Mozambique, and for a period of time in Cambodia.[3] In other cases, the move toward elections precipitated renewed conflict. This result occurred in Angola, in earlier peace efforts in Liberia, and to some extent in Rwanda. In Bosnia and Ethiopia, the move toward quick elections promoted the premature closing of the transition and the consolidation of power by leaders and institutions with dubious commitments to democracy or capacity to manage conflict. In other cases, such as the 1997 transition in Liberia, the elections served more as a mechanism of war termination with only a secondary and limited relationship to democratization.

In order to identify some of the factors that are related to the relative success of postconflict elections in achieving the dual goals of war termination and democratization, I will draw from the experiences of six cases—Angola (1992), Cambodia (1993), Mozambique (1994), El Salvador (1994), Bosnia (1996), and Liberia (1997)—where elections were a key event in the implementation process following a peace agreement to end a civil war. Elections have played other roles with relation to conflict management. They have served as a means to legitimate new political authority in the absence of a comprehensive peace agreement (Nicaragua, Sierra Leone); as a way to consolidate the military victory of one party (Ethiopia, Uganda); as an event that sparked or reignited conflict (Algeria, Burundi); and as a mechanism for conflict management and democraticization in internal conflicts that did not reach the threshold of civil war (South Africa, Haiti).[4] The explicit use of elections to implement peace agreements in the six cases under consideration here most clearly raises the issue of the relationship between the dual goals of war termination and democratization.

As these cases suggest, elections have become the principal means to legitimate the new leadership and institutional structures that emerge from a negotiated settlement to a civil war. Furthermore, the reliance on this mechanism is demonstrated by calls for elections as a key component of proposed war termination strategies in such places as the Democratic Republic of Congo (former Zaire/Kinshasa), the Republic of Congo (Brazzaville), Burundi, and Tajikistan. Such postconflict elections, however, carry a tremendous burden. They are called upon to settle the contentious issues of internal and external legitimacy and must be organized under the difficult circumstances of societal disorder, general insecurity, and institutional breakdown. In some cases they are expected to do the impossible: elections cannot settle a military conflict that negotiations have failed to end. An election designed to implement a peace agreement can be only as effective as the agreement itself.

Scholars and officials involved in policy toward El Salvador, Mozambique, Cambodia, Angola, and Bosnia have written a number of important monographs and articles on postconflict elections.[5] The recent Liberian election, however, has received little scholarly attention to date.[6] In addition, several recent studies have given a comparative perspective on international assistance to postconflict elections.[7] These studies have noted a number of characteristics that promote successful elections and have suggested conditions that should be in place before voting. However, less has been written on the distinctions between postconflict elections as ways to end a war and such elections as part of a process of democratization. Furthermore, little analysis exists on the options available when imperfect elections are the most credible alternative to a return to war.

There is a gap between analyses of conflict management and studies of political transitions. Specialists on conflict resolution have given more attention to the processes by which peace agreements are reached than to the implementation phase.[8] Scholars of democratization have argued that the nature of the old regime strongly influences the outcome of the transition.[9] For a state trying to complete a transition following destructive internal conflict, one of the most important characteristics of the transition will be the distortion or collapse of peacetime political institutions and social structures. A large and well-developed body of scholarship and expertise focuses on the political economy of transitions to political pluralism and market-oriented reform.[10] Scholars have written extensively about the transition from war to peace and from various forms of authoritarianism to democracy, but less is known about the dual transitions to peace and democracy. Yet elections have become a common element of war termination strategies.

An election by itself cannot serve as a sufficient strategy for successful implementation of a negotiated agreement to end a civil war. A review of recent case studies suggests that a number of variables are critical for postconflict elections to promote both war termination and democratization. These include the stage of the conflict and its "ripeness" at the time of the settlement; the nature of the settlement and transitional institutions (particularly interim security provisions and power-sharing arrangements); the character of the parties to the conflict (particularly the extent to which militias have been transformed into political parties before voting); the capacity of civil society to operate openly and participate effectively; the quality of the transitional authority and the existence of institutions that promote continuing negotiations and joint decisionmaking during the period between the cease-fire and elections; and the effectiveness of international support for implementation. If one or another of these conditions is unfavorable, elections may set back the peace process, disrupt democratization, or both. Instead of facilitating the creations of new, legitimate regimes, ineffective elections may either spark renewed fighting or sanction nondemocratic forces.

From the perspective of the international community, postconflict elections sometimes serve purposes not directly related to either conflict resolution or democratization. Policymakers in Washington and elsewhere often regard such elections as an important element in a strategy to disengage from a troublesome client (most notably in Cambodia, Angola, and Nicaragua) or as part of the exit strategy from a multilateral intervention (most notably in Bosnia and Liberia). In addition, international financial institutions and bilateral donors require a legitimate state in order to have a partner with whom to engage in programs of postwar reconstruction.[11] An election may "succeed" in the eyes of some policymakers if it allows disengagement or creates some kind of recognized authority with which to begin economic relations regardless of the elections' implications for sustained conflict management or democratization.

Postconflict elections are called upon to implement a peace agreement and therefore must be evaluated in the first instance against that goal. If the peace agreement is flawed and establishes an inappropriate framework for sustained conflict management or democratization, the quality of the election that finalizes the implementation process is unlikely to succeed in meeting these goals. Finally, in some circumstances, postconflict elections may have the potential to contribute to war termination but not democratization. In such cases, as will be the focus of the Liberian case study below, it may be a "least bad" policy to support elections for this more limited but still vitally important purpose.

IMPLEMENTING PEACE AGREEMENTS

Studies of conflict resolution suggest that mediated settlements to end internal conflicts are rare and that most civil wars end in "elimination or capitulation" of one or another party.[12] As I. William Zartman has argued, "Internal conflicts—civil wars—are the most difficult conflicts to negotiate."[13] Charles King describes the policy options for the international community in stark terms: "Judging from historical evidence, then, the choice for external powers seems to be between allowing civil wars to 'run their course' and risk massive levels of human suffering and physical destruction, or to promote a negotiated settlement which, if it can ever be reached, may be inherently unstable."[14] In some important cases, however, parties have reached a point of "mutually hurting stalemate" whereby the combatants determine that a negotiated settlement is better than unilateral options and the conflict becomes "ripe" for resolution through mediation.[15] Ripeness is a notoriously difficult condition to operationalize or even to recognize except in hindsight.[16] In many cases of internal conflict, however, outsiders have played important roles in hastening the "ripening" process by applying pressures, floating ideas, proffering inducements, setting deadlines, and discouraging unilateral moves.[17]

Nature of the Agreement

Even when conditions are ripe, negotiated agreements to end internal wars are by their nature imperfect documents. The settlements, signed under pressures to reach a cease-fire and end humanitarian suffering, generally include what they can, leave out what cannot be settled, and gloss over differences in an effort to stop the killing. The commitment and intentions of various actors are unclear until tested by a peace process. Mediators may emphasize best-case scenarios (or even engage in wishful thinking) to convince nervous parties to accept the risks of laying down their arms and pursuing their objectives nonviolently. This is perhaps sensible or even inevitable as a first step toward conflict management, but issues unaddressed or obscured in peace agreements often return to haunt the implementation process. As a result, as Fen Osler Hampson states, "Peace agreement[s] sometimes contain the seeds of their own destruction."[18]

Because the international community cannot in any real sense "guarantee" peace agreements in internal conflicts, the agreements must be largely self-enforcing.[19] In a number of cases, peace agreements have broken down before or immediately after elections were held. The 1994 Arusha Agreements in Rwanda collapsed when extremist Hutu groups, intent on preventing the transition, launched genocide following the plane crash that killed President Juvenal Habyarimana.[20] The Liberian civil war saw several peace agreements collapse before elections could get off the drawing board between 1990 and 1996, in part because of insufficient demilitarization and the formation of new factions seeking their piece of the pie. In Angola, Jonas Savimbi refused to demobilize much of his insurgent Uniao Nacional pela Independencia Total de Angola (UNITA) force, defected from the 1992 peace agreement, and returned to war when it became apparent that he had lost the elections. In cases where the peace process collapses before elections, the flaws in the agreement are made tragically clear. In other cases, when the process collapses following elections, the degree to which the settlement or the electoral phase of implementation is to blame is more difficult to judge.

Interim Governments

While in hindsight it is often clear that a particular peace agreement was not suited to a specific conflict, other peace processes, such as in

Mozambique and El Salvador, also appeared doomed at first but succeeded in the end. As noted, transitional periods and interim institutions supported by the international community may create dynamics that strengthen forces with an interest in peace and weaken extremists and spoilers. In any case, the period between the signing of an agreement and an election provides the context for testing and assessing the risks and benefits of cooperation and the intentions and commitments of each party. How the transitional period is managed, what interim institutions are created, how the inevitable security dilemmas are addressed, and what time and resources are available for the transition will shape the potential for the elections to serve as an instrument to promote war termination and democratization.

Interim governments are by their nature not legitimated by democratic institutions but derive their authority from the extent to which they prepare the country for meaningful elections and turn power over to the winners.[21] In the meantime, however, the country needs to be governed. Critical and contentious policies must be made on developing an electoral framework, implementing demilitarization, reintegrating the displaced, and reestablishing functioning economic and legal institutions. The process through which such decisions are made will shape the expectations of the major actors and may inspire confidence or ignite fears.

Postconflict interim governments may be established by peace agreements in many ways. Governments of national reconciliation in which most if not all of the major parties participate may be the most conducive to a successful outcome. In South Africa, a process of extensive negotiations resulted in an interim government of national unity and norms of power sharing that guided the country's transition.[22] In other cases, such as Mozambique and El Salvador, there is some promise in a less institutionalized regime with an array of technocratic joint committees charged with managing such issues as demobilization and monitoring the cease-fire, supported by an effective international presence. In Cambodia, large dimensions of what is generally within the purview of a sovereign state's internal affairs came under UN authority. In Bosnia, the international peacekeeping forces and administrators from the Organization for Security and Cooperation in Europe (OSCE) also assumed critical functions when no agreement could be reached for local administration.

Some interim regimes have been organized around implicit or explicit political "pacts," a set of negotiated compromises among competing elites with the goal of institutionalizing the distribution of power and reducing uncertainty.[23] For transitional regimes established to administer postconflict elections, the key elements of the pacts are provisions for demilitarization and electoral rules. If agreement on interim institutions based on broad power sharing is possible, then the prospects for an acceptable election are enhanced. Such power-sharing arrangements may be the best attainable short-term goal compatible with long-term democratization.[24]

Because policies enacted during a transitional period will inevitably provoke conflict, interim governments need well-developed institutions to manage such disputes. A well-constructed peace agreement generally includes provisions for ongoing negotiations and bargaining, thereby building norms of nonviolent governance that may reinforce the momentum for successful democratization.[25] In Mozambique, for example, the General Peace Agreement "had laid the foundation stone, but the construction of a lasting peace in Mozambique required still more negotiation and planning."[26] Disputes among parties are inevitable in the transitional period as the broad principles listed in the peace agreement must be made operational and relevant in a difficult and tense atmosphere. A process of collaborative problem solving among the parties to the agreement will foster confidence and legitimize the decisions.

In a number of cases, special commissions were established during the transitional period. In El Salvador, the 1991 New York accords led to the creation of a National Commission for the Consolidation of Peace (COPAZ), a body with representation from the government, the Farabundo Marti National Liberation Front (FMLN) insurgents, and each of the parties in the National Assembly.[27] COPAZ worked as a "makeshift attempt at a transitory government."[28] In Mozambique, the Supervision and Control Commission brought together the major political actors with the major donors in a consultative process chaired by the special representative of the UN secretary general. Other specialized commissions dealt with cease-fire monitoring, reintegration of ex-combatants, reform of the Mozambican defense forces, and preparations for the election.[29]

Angola and the early attempts in Liberia demonstrate that poorly constructed peace agreements may lead to transitional arrangements that fail to build the confidence or joint decisionmaking that is associated with power sharing and a well-managed transition. Under the 1991 Bicesse Accords in Angola, pro forma meetings among the parties within the Joint Political-Military Commission did not act to change behavior and may have created a false sense of confidence in the parties' commitment.[30] Under the Yamoussoukro and Cotonou agreements in Liberia, interim administration was parceled out to each of the factions with only a weak and generally stalemated Council of State assigned the impossible job of coordination.

Managing the Security Dilemma

Some of the most difficult challenges to an internal peace agreement are the inevitable security dilemmas among the combatants.[31] Government and insurgent leaders alike must make difficult judgments about the likely costs and benefits of accepting the agreement under conditions of imperfect information about the goals and character of their opponents. Rogue elements have the capacity to destroy the process.[32] As Stephen Stedman has stated, "By signing a peace agreement, leaders put themselves at risk from adversaries who may take advantage of a settlement, from disgruntled followers who see peace as a betrayal of key values, and from excluded parties who seek either to alter the process or to destroy it."[33] Barbara Walker similarly has written that peace agreements in civil wars ask opponents "to do what they consider unthinkable. At a time when no legitimate government and no legal institutions exist to enforce a contract, they are asked to demobilize, disarm, and disengage their military forces and prepare for peace."[34]

A settlement of an internal war, unless it results in partition, generally includes provisions for demobilization of fighters and the creation of a new national army and police force. Because of the pervasive distrust among the parties and the high risk of demobilizing one's forces if your rival cheats and does not, such provisions are notoriously difficult to implement. Nearly all parties hedge and keep some portion of their fighters and weapons outside the demobilization process. The fact that disarmament is inherently imperfect need not prevent implementation if the political dimensions of the peace process are adequate. Aldo Ajello, the special representative in charge of the UN operation in Mozambique, realistically appraised the options:

> I know very well that they will give us old and obsolete material, and they will have here and there something hidden. I don't care. What I do is create the political situation in which the use of those guns is not the question. So that they stay where they are.[35]

In addition to the security dilemmas inherent in a process of demilitarization without established institutions to monitor compliance, a transition ending in elections has at its core an element of risk. As Adam Przeworski has argued, the essence of democratic elections is that "no one can be certain that their interests will ultimately triumph."[36] On the other hand, if everything is at stake in a postconflict election, it will be difficult to convince parties that retain a military option to accept the results. This leads to a situation where postconflict elections should decide something but not too much.[37] It is to reduce uncertainty and thereby create security and a willingness to comply that makes political pacts useful in transitions. Pacts, however, ultimately rely upon other mechanisms for enforcement and do not by themselves end uncertainty or resolve the security dilemma.

Moderates willing to engage in cooperative behavior are particularly vulnerable to outbidding by extremists and are hostage to spoilers and rejectionists who can derail the process. Building a coalition of support to bolster those in favor of the agreement is therefore imperative. According to Timothy Sisk,

> A necessary condition for the mitigation of conflict in deeply divided societies is the existence, or creation, of a centrist core of moderates—drawn both from elites and from the broader civil society—that adheres to rules and norms of pragmatic coexistence with other groups and can withstand the pressures of extremist outbidders that seek to mobilize on divisive themes for their own power-seeking aims.[38]

If moderates cannot withstand the pressures from more militant elements, the agreement will likely fail, as happened in Rwanda in 1994.

Interim periods are important times for testing the intentions and commitments of the major actors who seek to play a role in the politics of the postconflict state.[39] In many cases, warring parties, such as the Khmer Rouge in Cambodia, UNITA in Angola, and Charles

Taylor's National Patriotic Front of Liberia, hoped to win through the transitional process what they perceived they could not win on the battlefield and were prepared to abandon the agreement and return to war if they determined they would lose. Such parties are likely to view elections in an instrumental way and be ready to adopt undemocratic methods or reengage in warfare rather than lose. In other cases, such as El Salvador, Nicaragua, and Mozambique (after a last-minute threat to boycott), parties that had been engaged in conflict were prepared to take the risk and participate in elections either because they were confident they would win (but were prepared to accept the consequences of losing) or because they recognized that they could not win militarily. In a third set of cases, the willingness of a potential spoiler to accept defeat was untested because the party in question won the contest, as in Liberia in 1997, or forced a postelection power-sharing arrangement, as in Cambodia.

Demilitarizing Politics

Also critical to the successful implementation of an agreement that culminates in meaningful elections are the transformation of the warring militias into effective political parties and the development of a political community capable of supporting democratization. In the long term, it is extremely difficult for militias to play the role of competing political parties in a democratic system if they remain organized and led as they were during the period of armed conflict. The problem is particularly difficult for insurgents who regard themselves as national liberation movements.[40] In many cases the old regime also needs to move from authoritarian to democratic structures appropriate for peaceful electoral competition. Finally, the general population needs the time and security to return to their homes and reestablish their communities and the structures of civil society necessary to support democracy.

A crucial ingredient in this transformation of political organizations is demilitarization. If the militias and armed forces are convinced to give up their weapons and permit neutral bodies to control security, they are far more likely to pursue their aims through political contestation. Interim security may be managed by joint forces of the former combatants or by an international or regional peacekeeping operation.

Demilitarization requires significant resources to enable demobilized soldiers to find work, return to their farms, and reintegrate into civilian society.[41] The critical characteristic of successful demilitarization with regard to meaningful elections is the extent to which military options are made less likely, convincing parties and voters that the results of the election will hold. Demilitarization may serve as a critical test of a militia's willingness to accept the new political institutions and processes included in the peace agreement. If a faction refuses to demilitarize, the risk of defection from the agreement is high and democratic elections are difficult to conduct.

In El Salvador, the insurgent FMLN successfully participated in a UN-supervised process of demobilization and converted itself to an officially registered political party.[42] The United Nations recognized that the FMLN's "transformation into a political party and the full reintegration of its members . . . into the civil, political and institutional life of the country, are at the very core of the Peace Accords."[43] In Mozambique, the international community provided considerable resources and incentives to a trust fund to encourage the insurgent Mozambique National Resistance (Renamo) to transform itself from a military organization to a political party.[44] In Cambodia, the Royalist coalition (United National Front for an Independent, Neutral, Peaceful and Cooperative Cambodia, FUNCINPEC) developed into a political party while the Khmer Rouge continued to operate as a guerrilla movement throughout the electoral period. In Angola, UNITA never made the transformation to a political party. Ethiopian politico-military organizations, including the Ethiopian Peoples Revolutionary Democratic Front and the Oromo Liberation Front, continued to be structured and commanded as military organizations during the failed 1992 elections and to an extent thereafter.[45] In Liberia, as discussed below, the skill and ease by which the National Patriotic Front for Liberia transformed itself from an insurgent military organization into the populist National Patriotic Party suggests that some skills and structures developed during the armed struggle can be used as the base for an effective political organization.

In addition to providing a relatively level playing field for the ex-combatants to compete as political parties, a successful agreement should provide opportunity for political organizations or parties that seek to mobilize constituencies not engaged in the fighting. Such organizations may be new political parties or old organizations that had been banned or were operating underground. A peace agreement that fosters a more democratic and sustainable political order should be more than an agreement among militias to divide up the spoils.

In many cases, however, parties not connected to former military organizations have been permitted to compete but have had a difficult time winning support with limited resources in the polarized context of a postconflict election. In Angola, Mozambique, Bosnia, and Liberia, dozens of small civilian-based parties competed but won only token support compared with the parties of the former combatants. In a context where major assets, most notably the media, have been captured by warring factions and control or even access to the countryside is in the hands of the militias, the playing field will be decidedly tilted against civilian parties. In addition, the insecurity that characterizes a postconflict society, particularly if the cease-fire is recent, will lead large numbers of voters to support the more militant and often chauvinistic candidates, as was demonstrated in Bosnia and Liberia. Finally, in the context of a civil war, militia leaders often are regarded by significant civilian constituencies as protectors or liberators, not as warlords lacking legitimacy.

A civil society capable of playing its essential role in a political system based on electoral competition needs time and security to develop out of the very different structures that characterize war-torn societies. Civilian institutions and leaders suffer the brunt of internal conflict. War-torn societies are characterized by suspicion, polarization, small-scale and parochial institutions, and defensive organizations. A militarized society develops institutions and leaders that are not suitable for a peacetime society or sustained democratization. Conflicts generate specific societal rhythms and patterns of behavior that clash with the social formations needed to support movement toward democracy. Societies distorted by conflict have different rules, structures, cultures, and psychological demands than peacetime societies. The structures of war therefore need to be replaced with routinized and institutionalized patterns of peaceful interactions.[46]

During the period of conflict and the insecurity immediately following a cease-fire, nonmilitary leaders will be less likely to step forward and build the organizations, propose the ideas, and demonstrate the capacity to lead that a peaceful political system requires. A period of time for new leaders to develop their programs and build links to their constituencies will be necessary. A population that disengaged from the formal political process during the period of conflict will need to be incorporated again. The process of addressing collective grievances, selecting legitimate spokespersons, forging and reforging social alliances, and creating local and national organizations takes time, and progress will likely proceed on the basis of three steps forward, two steps back.[47] Insecurity breeds distrust and favors the most ruthless over those most willing to build consensus and to compromise. If the transition creates an environment that allows civilian elements that had not been engaged in the conflict in an organized manner to step forward and participate, voters will have a greater choice and the results are more likely to be meaningful to the population and thereby promote democratization.

Timing of Elections

In many cases, rather than a quick transition that locks in place new institutions and leaders through elections, a longer period of flexible, interim administration has a greater potential to encourage the social and political institutions capable of sustaining a transition to democracy, as was the case in El Salvador and Mozambique. Until some semblance of a state can be reconstructed and civil society given the time, security, and space to rebuild, elections may reignite conflict (as in Angola) or lead to a premature closing of politics by legitimizing nondemocratic forces (as in Ethiopia, Bosnia, and Liberia). A period of fluidity in which new organizations have time to build support, rather than a rapid process of solidifying the structures and institutions that developed during the conflict, will lay the social foundations that can support effective elections and competitive politics. A transitional arrangement in which the timing of an election is tied to conditions on the ground rather than an artificial date enshrined in advance in a peace accord has a greater chance of succeeding. In Mozambique, such an open-ended election date frustrated the international community that financed the transition but probably resulted in a better election and more sustainable outcome.

In a number of cases, however, such lengthy transitions are likely to be impossible because the nature of the conflict, the continuing belief by one or more parties that they can win militarily, the ineffectiveness of the interim regime, and the lack of political will and resources from the international community to support a more drawn-out transition may require quick elections.[48] If the peace agreement is unlikely to hold for a sustained transitional period, then it may be necessary to hold the elections before putting in place an enabling environment likely to support democratization. In such cases, the postconflict elections may advance war termination but are unlikely to contribute in a significant way to democratization.

In several cases, it seems unlikely that additional time would have improved the prospects for a more democratic outcome. In Angola, a longer transition that did not change the fundamental flaws of the peace agreement or build a method to contain Savimbi's threat as a spoiler probably would not have changed the outcome. The short-comings in the Bosnian election were tied fundamentally to the Dayton Accords and international policy and also would not have been changed substantially by delay.[49] In Liberia, the dysfunctional nature of the interim institutions and the unwillingness of the regional peacekeepers or the broader international community to support a longer transition made it imperative to hold elections quickly after the cease-fire.

As will be suggested by the analysis of the Liberian case below, if a sustained transition is not possible given the nature of the peace process, the contending parties, or international or regional interventions, then a relatively rapid election to promote war termination may be the best (or "least bad") outcome. To insist that postconflict elections should not be held until the enabling environment of democratization is in place may mean missing an opportunity to help end the war and could thus lead the country back into conflict. In some cases war termination and democratization may go together, but in other cases it may be necessary to achieve an end to the fighting first and then initiate a process of democratization.

2

The Liberian Civil War: Regional Intervention and Failed Peacemaking

Postconflict elections to implement peace agreements following civil war have dual objectives—to promote war termination and to advance democratization. As outlined in chapter 1, in some cases both objectives have been met, but in others only war termination was achieved, or neither was accomplished. The nature of the peace agreement and the interim institutions developed to manage the transition shape the relative success or failure of such elections in relation to these twin goals.

The Liberian case illustrates a number of these dimensions. The war ended with one faction, Charles Taylor's National Patriotic Front for Liberia (NPFL), still strong and still convinced that it could achieve its objectives through unilateral military moves if the transitional process threatened to weaken its position. After twelve failed agreements, the West African–sponsored Abuja peace process represented an effort to end the fighting and allow the West African peacekeeping troops to withdraw as quickly as possible. War termination and disengagement goals rather than democratization were uppermost in the minds of the leaders who negotiated the agreement and managed its implementation. The fundamental causes of the conflict, rooted in overly centralized and unchecked political power, failed to receive attention. The Abuja settlement represented a minimal process to end the immediate fighting without addressing the underlying political challenges that both launched the war and that needed to be addressed to create a context of enduring peace and democratization.

In addition, the Liberian case demonstrates the difficulties created by poorly designed and supported transitional institutions. The interim government and transitional processes established by the Abuja Accord created very weak institutions, stalemated by their competing factional composition. The rival parties had few opportunities to engage in multilateral talks regarding the administration of the interim period or to build a sense of confidence. Demilitarization of combatants, repatriation of refugees, and rebuilding civil society and political parties received lesser priority than ending the fighting. Little attention was paid to the problems of an unlevel political playing field or building a peacetime society before elections.

Some of these problems are related to the ambiguous attitudes of the international community toward the peace process in Liberia. The international community was divided between the Economic Community of West African States (ECOWAS), determined to find a mechanism that would allow them to disengage from Liberia while winning credit for ending the war, and the broader international donor community, interested in limiting its involvement and demonstrating the capacity of regional organizations to manage protracted conflicts that the United Nations did not want to engage.[1] The Liberian transition represented an experiment in international peacekeeping, whereby a regional organization, in this case ECOWAS, served as the leading organization charged with managing the process with a mandate from the United Nations as envisioned in chapter VIII of the UN Charter. International concerns regarding Nigeria's true agenda, on the one hand, and a desire to demonstrate the validity of regional peace operations, on the other, pulled the donor community in two directions, leaving it with a confused purpose in Liberia.

As a result of these factors, the Liberian transition ended in an election that accomplished the minimal goal of bringing to power a new national leader. The process, however, ratified power alignments created by seven years of war rather than representing a meaningful exercise of choice. In addition to this limited contribution to democratization, the process of "railroading peace," raised serious concerns regarding its sustainability.[2] With the fundamental issues relating to the distribution of power and the means by which misuse of power might be checked unresolved, the Abuja peace process risked creating a short-lived interregnum between periods of instability.

CIVIL WAR AND REGIONAL PEACEKEEPING

On Christmas Eve 1989, an armed incursion led by Charles Taylor and one hundred or so followers organized as the National Patriotic Front for Liberia (NPFL) entered northern Liberia from Côte d'Ivoire to overthrow the authoritarian and ineffective government of Samuel Doe.[3] The ensuing conflict degenerated into such brutality that the state collapsed and social structures became distorted almost beyond recognition. Between 1990 and 1997, one-tenth of the prewar population of 2.5 million died, one-third became refugees, and nearly all of the rest had been displaced at one time or another.[4] Motivated in part by the destabilizing threat the conflict represented to West Africa, the Economic Community of West African States (ECOWAS) created the ECOWAS Cease-Fire Monitoring Group (ECOMOG) and intervened with military force in an effort to end the conflict. In August 1996 the final of thirteen peace agreements was signed in Abuja, Nigeria. The Abuja Accord called for a rapid transition ending in elections.

The Old Order and Doe's Regime

Liberia's unique political history was shaped by the quasi-colonial nature of its relationship with the United States as a territory settled in the nineteenth century in part by freed slaves from the southern United States, a group whose descendants are known as Americo-Liberians. U.S. influence expanded in the twentieth century as major U.S. companies opened massive rubber estates and the United States built military facilities and a Voice of America relay station near Monrovia. In 1942 the two states signed a Defense Areas Agreement that committed the United States to defend Liberian sovereignty and authorized Washington to construct and defend military airbases in Liberia during World War II.

The Americo-Liberian oligarchy exercised political control through the True Whig Party and economic dominance through interlocking family ties in business and professional life.[5] Opposition to these privileges began to be organized among intellectuals and university professors in the late 1970s. In 1979 President William Tolbert increased the price of rice—the staple food for most Liberians—by 50 percent, unleashing a wave of demonstrations and riots. Leading these demonstrations were several intellectuals who continued to play critical roles in Liberia through 1997. The Movement for Justice in Africa (MOJA), led by Amos Sawyer, Togba-Nah Tipoteh, and H. Boima Fahnbulleh Jr., and the Progressive Alliance of Liberia (PAL), led by Gabriel Baccus Matthews, stepped forward to lead the opposition.[6] Tolbert's government vacillated and demonstrated weakness in response to the Rice Riots. With the True Whig Party and the intellectual leaders of the opposition clashing, the military stepped into the vacuum. The end to the old order finally and dramatically came on April 12, 1980, when a group of noncommissioned officers led by Master Sergeant Samuel Doe seized power and publicly executed a number of the old elite.[7]

To build legitimacy and in response to pressures from the United States, the military government revised the constitution, held a referendum to adopt the new document, and organized multiparty elections. During the period leading up to the October 1985 election, however, Doe harassed and eventually disqualified a number of political opponents from participating and used his control over state patronage and the media to dominate the campaign. In a precedent that continued to resonate in 1997, Liberian voters overcame their fears of the authoritarian state and voted decisively for the opposition. After early returns indicated that Doe was losing the vote, he conspired to win through fraud. Doe appointed a hand-picked, partisan committee to conduct ballot counting in secret. Two weeks after the voting, the official results were announced: Samuel Doe "won" 50.9 percent in the four-way race for the presidency.[8] Few Liberians or other international observers believed these results.[9] Most maintained that Jackson Doe (no relation) had in fact won the most votes.

In the aftermath, a failed coup by General Thomas Quiwonkpa led to massive reprisals against the Gio and Mano peoples in Nimba County, who were perceived as supporting the coup.[10] Over time, it became increasingly clear that the regime relied upon military force, dominated by Doe's Krahn ethnic brethren, to remain in power. Doe's revised constitution had strengthened the powers of the presidency and limited the ability of the legislature and the courts to challenge him. Repression and arrests of opposition politicians, independent journalists, and others allegedly involved with Doe's rivals dominated the late 1980s. Without any mechanisms to permit peaceful challenges to Doe's rule, an economic crisis as international donors withdrew, and with growing repression that took on ethnic dimensions, a violent crisis seemed difficult to avoid.

The United States recognized these worrisome trends but continued to perceive Doe's Liberia as an important client in global cold war strategies. In addition to the military and communications facilities based near Monrovia, U.S. intelligence services used Liberia to monitor Libya and to assist UNITA rebels in Angola.[11] U.S. financial support increased in the mid-1980s as President Ronald Reagan began to use assistance, and particularly military assistance, to reward those states that supported Washington's global agenda, regardless of their domestic policies or human rights records. By the late 1980s, however, growing instability within Liberia, the technical obsolescence of some of the military facilities, and growing criticism regarding U.S.-Liberian relations from Congress and from human rights groups such as Africa Watch led Washington to cut aid and begin to disengage from the country.[12]

Civil War, State Collapse, and Regional Peacekeeping

In 1989 an insurgent force known as the National Patriotic Front of Liberia (NPFL) led by Charles Taylor, a former official in Doe's regime, entered Nimba County. The core of the NPFL included Libyan-trained soldiers, supplemented by adventurers, professional revolutionaries, and mercenaries from across West Africa. Doe's Armed Forces of Liberia (AFL), dominated by ethnic Krahn and supported by some Mandingo leaders, unleashed a scorched earth campaign in Nimba County, terrorizing civilian Gio and Mano ethnic groups. These populations, already traumatized as a result of the reprisals following the 1985 Quiwonkpa coup attempt, rallied to the NPFL cause. The AFL pushed large segments of the population into the NPFL camp, and the insurgents subsequently advanced rapidly, reaching the outskirts of Monrovia by July 1990.[13]

The United States sent a warship with 2,000 marines to West Africa, and many Liberians expected an intervention by the country with which it had such close and long-standing ties. Instead, the marines stuck to their mandate and evacuated U.S. nationals from Monrovia while avoiding involvement in the conflict. The Department of State's Africa Bureau made tentative efforts to encourage Doe and his closest supporters to leave Liberia and initially was willing to accept what they regarded as Taylor's inevitable take-over. The White House, however, was reluctant to take responsibility for such a transition and Washington kept its distance from the crisis.[14] In part, with the cold war over, Washington had less interest in who (if anyone) controlled Liberia. In addition, Iraq's invasion of Kuwait in August 1990 shifted attention to that military threat in a far more important region. Many Liberians, however, were disappointed in the decision not to intervene and suggested that such an intervention would have been welcomed by the overwhelming majority who wanted peace.[15]

Chaos in the capital—with widespread looting, ethnic killings, and, in one particularly indelible incident, the murder of 600 displaced persons under Red Cross protection in a Lutheran church by the AFL[16]—convinced Liberia's neighbors in the Economic Community of West African States (ECOWAS) to act. The ECOWAS Standing Mediation Committee, an ad hoc group composed of Gambia, Ghana, Nigeria, Togo, and Mali with a vague mandate, declared a cease-fire and established the ECOWAS Cease-Fire Monitoring Group (ECOMOG). The operation began and largely remained a Nigerian initiative presented to the rest of the region as a fait accompli, without a working consensus from the broader region.[17] In addition to its concerns about regional stability, Nigeria saw the Liberian crisis as an opportunity to demonstrate its leadership in West Africa. African leaders insisted on handling the crisis regionally and opposed attempts to place the Liberian crisis on the United Nations Security Council agenda (much to the relief of the United States and other members of the Security Council who did not want to engage the difficult issue).[18]

According to its mandate, ECOMOG's purpose was "keeping the peace, restoring law and order and ensuring that the cease-fire is respected."[19] This peacekeeping mandate, however, never matched the situation on the ground where there was not even a cease-fire. The open-ended nature of the intervention and the emphasis on elections as the mechanism of war termination was made clear by ECOMOG's declaration that it "shall remain in Liberia, if necessary, until the successful holding of general elections and the installation of an elected government."[20] Taylor rejected the ECOWAS peace initiative from the start, arguing that it shored up Doe's tottering regime and denied him the position he had earned.[21] As a result, ECOMOG quickly adopted a peace-enforcement mission. ECOMOG troops landed in Monrovia's port on August 24 and were attacked by Taylor's NPFL forces when they tried to move toward the center of the city the next day.[22]

Shortly thereafter, ECOWAS sponsored peace talks in Banjul, The Gambia in August 1990. Taylor and the NPFL refused to participate, reiterating their contention that ECOWAS was not a neutral party to the conflict. Regardless, the Banjul meeting selected Amos Sawyer to head an Interim Government of National Unity (IGNU) and, in a pattern that would be followed in subsequent agreements, called for elections within twelve months. In early September, Doe was captured and brutally killed by a breakaway faction of the NPFL led by Prince Yormie Johnson.[23] The removal of Doe did not settle the question of who would be the next legitimate president.

ECOMOG then began a military campaign that succeeded in driving Taylor back from Monrovia. In November 1990, Taylor and representatives of Johnson and the AFL signed a cease-fire in Bamako, Mali. The Bamako Agreement again called for the holding of presidential and general elections within twelve months. The agreement created a situation of uneasy peace with "Greater Monrovia" governed by IGNU and protected by ECOMOG while the rest of the country was controlled by Charles Taylor and what he called the National Patriotic Reconstruction Assembly Government (NPRAG) based in Gbarnga in northern Liberia.[24] Neither government recognized the other. ECOMOG could not defeat the NPFL, and Taylor would not accept the ECOWAS-created IGNU as the framework for a transitional government.

Washington, Liberia's traditional patron, continued to keep its distance from the developing crisis. The United States, alone among Western countries, kept its embassy in Monrovia open, enabling it to play a diplomatic role. Washington's policy focused on hortatory support for the ECOWAS peace process and statements designed to reinforce regional leadership (and avoid significant or controversial U.S. involvement). National Security Adviser Brent Scowcroft suggested that "it was difficult to see how we could intervene without taking over and pacifying the country," a level of involvement that had few advocates in Washington.[25] International news during the summer of 1990 was dominated by the Iraqi invasion of Kuwait and, with the exception of a few sensational reports on massacres, Liberia received little public attention. Liberia was reported as a "lower order, weird African war."[26] Washington chose to treat Liberia as a humanitarian problem and ignored what some regarded as an opportunity to play a constructive diplomatic role.[27] Assistant Secretary of State for African Affairs Herman J. Cohen later stated, "We missed an opportunity in Liberia. . . . We did not intervene either militarily or diplomatically."[28]

ECOWAS therefore managed the peace process. Additional meetings took place in Lomé, Togo (February 1991), and Yamoussoukro, Côte d'Ivoire (five meetings between June and October 1991). Each of these meetings called for a cease-fire, demobilization, and a transitional period culminating in elections. None was implemented.[29] An All Liberia National Conference was held near Monrovia from March through April 1991 and succeeded at first in getting the major parties to talk, but the NPFL eventually walked out of the meeting. Former U.S. President Jimmy Carter's International Negotiation Network became involved in promoting the talks and offered to assist in the organization and observation of elections, but each of the agreements failed in the early phases of implementation.

Taylor continued to distrust ECOWAS and Nigerian intentions and resisted turning his weapons over to ECOMOG as stipulated in the various peace agreements. Although these various talks took place during 1991, armed clashes continued in many parts of Liberia and the war spread as the NPFL made incursions into Sierra Leone in April. The NPFL provided assistance and encouragement to an insurgent group in Sierra Leone known as the Revolutionary United Front (RUF). Taylor sought to weaken Sierra Leone's commitment to ECOMOG and interfere with the ECOMOG advance logistics base in Sierra Leone, as well as gain control over lucrative diamond-producing areas. The peace agreements and cease-fires adopted by ECOWAS seemed disconnected to the dynamics of warfare and economic networks on the ground.

The Yamoussoukro Agreement

The October 1991 meeting resulted in the Yamoussoukro IV Agreement, the most fully developed peace accord of the series. Under this agreement, the NPFL and the AFL made a commitment to encamp their forces and disarm to ECOMOG by January 15, 1992, and to participate in quick elections scheduled for spring 1992. As with previous agreements, however, these provisions were never implemented. The election commission stated that it would not hold elections until encampment and disarming of factional forces were realized.[30] The failure to implement the agreement occurred in part because of the emergence of new factions, such as the United Liberation Movement of Liberia for Democracy (ULIMO, established by Krahn and Mandingo former AFL members). ULIMO emerged in western Liberia with the backing of the Sierra Leone government in retaliation for Taylor's support of RUF and with support by others in ECOWAS who sought local allies to join in the effort to defeat the NPFL.[31] In addition, implementation of Yamoussoukro IV stalled because the NPFL used the agreement tactically as a breathing space to rearm and relaunch attacks designed to win unilaterally. Taylor believed he could outlast ECOMOG and win on his own terms.[32] Finally, tensions within ECOWAS between Nigeria and its Francophone neighbors hampered the organization responsible for implementation. While Nigeria, Sierra Leone, and others sought to defeat the NPFL, Côte d'Ivoire and Burkina Faso continued to support Taylor.

Taylor, ruling 95 percent of Liberia from his capital in Gbarnga, managed his own currency and banking system, his own radio network, and engaged in international trade in diamonds, gold, rubber, and timber. He made deals with rubber plantation owners, sold iron ore to the British firm African Mining Consortium and the French-owned Sollac, and became the third largest supplier of tropical timber to France.[33] IGNU President Amos Sawyer complained that "for all practical purposes Mr. Taylor is conducting a clearance sale of Liberia's resources."[34] Revenues from such trade went to support NPFL fighters and administrators and to purchase weapons on the international arms market, which was flooded with cheap weapons from the dismantled armies of eastern Europe. Taylor's forces reportedly killed a number of rival opposition politicians to consolidate their control, most notably Jackson Doe, the popularly recognized winner of the 1985 presidential election rigged by Samuel Doe.

Much of the fighting between the NPFL, ULIMO, and ECOMOG was over control of economic assets such as mines and ports that served to finance and sustain the armed factions. As Stephen Ellis describes the *"logique de guerre"*:

> The fighters were mostly not soldiers at all, but armed civilians, sometimes very young, who lived by the gun, stealing what they needed or wanted. . . . War-bands based themselves in any area where there were exploitable resources, especially diamond-producing areas, or where villagers were still producing crops, or places where humanitarian convoys could be looted. They would defend these strategic positions against all comers while raiding the territory of rival militias with the aim of looting, damaging the enemy's core population, and commandeering slave labour, in a way probably akin to the mode of warfare practiced in the days of the slave trade.[35]

Only rarely did organized military units confront one another. The war was largely fought between unarmed civilians and ruthless gangs of youths looking for booty or to secure economically important territory. The conflict was "a battle over commerce."[36]

Liberian militias often were unfed but well-armed children whose activities quickly degenerated into looting and terrorizing civilians.[37] One American reporter characterized the conflict as "at times unspeakably brutal and at other times surreal. It is a war in which field officers with names like General Mosquito command young combatants, high on drugs, who sometimes dress in women's wigs and wedding gowns and put on nail polish and Donald Duck masks before committing atrocities against members of opposing tribes."[38] A particularly brutal massacre took place in June 1993 when 500 displaced persons were killed at the former Firestone Rubber plantation in Harbel. Observers initially blamed the NPFL, but a UN-appointed commission of inquiry concluded that the massacre was carried out by the AFL.[39]

To broaden participation in ECOMOG, support the Yamoussoukro process, and respond to Taylor's fears of Nigeria, the United States provided assistance to and put pressure on Senegal to send a military contingent to Liberia in October 1991.[40] ECOMOG expanded and began to deploy in areas along Liberia's borders with Guinea and Sierra Leone to prevent the conflict from spreading. Deployment to areas controlled by the NPFL, however, was derailed by continued fighting between Taylor's forces and ULIMO. In May 1992, Senegalese peacekeepers were captured and executed by NPFL troops in northern Liberia, leading ECOMOG to withdraw its troops to

Monrovia.[41] Large-scale fighting between ULIMO and the NPFL during the summer of 1992 set off a new round of displacement. ULIMO, operating out of bases in Sierra Leone, gained control of large areas of Lofa and Grand Cape Mount counties in western Liberia. The deadline to encamp forces passed in an atmosphere of increased rather than reduced fighting.

Taylor stated that he would not disarm while fighting with ULIMO continued and "Sierra Leone and other ECOWAS countries continue to support ULIMO."[42] ECOWAS issued a communiqué in July 1992 condemning Taylor's obstructions and threatening "comprehensive sanctions" unless the terms of Yamoussoukro were implemented.[43] Tensions between Taylor and ECOMOG escalated, and the NPFL took ECOMOG troops hostage. These soldiers eventually were released after a visit by former U.S. President Jimmy Carter. Many were returned without their weapons, vehicles, or even their uniforms or personal belongings.[44] Talks could not move forward on a bilateral basis between the NPFL and Sawyer's interim government, while the growing importance of ULIMO indicated that the conflict was becoming increasingly multilateral.[45]

Operation Octopus

Taylor, frustrated with the peace process and convinced that the outcome of the war would be determined by military force, launched a major offensive known as Operation Octopus to seize Monrovia in October 1992. The NPFL leadership wanted to eliminate ULIMO and recognized that ULIMO soldiers had taken refuge behind ECOMOG lines around Monrovia. Taylor demanded that ECOMOG get out of the way and stop protecting his rivals. He stated that ECOMOG soldiers should "pull into their barracks and raise their white flags and let us mop up this thing and get it over with. . . . We can stop [the war] within the next few days if ECOMOG [will] get out of the way and let us complete this campaign. . . . We are going to continue this campaign until we liberate our citizens and Monrovia from ULIMO."[46]

In the ensuing warfare, five American nuns were murdered near their convent on the outskirts of Monrovia, another atrocity attributed to NPFL forces.[47] The NPFL shelled Monrovia and nearly captured the capital before a fierce counterattack by ECOMOG forces that included heavy artillery and naval bombardment of residential neighborhoods where NPFL forces were dug in.[48] In addition, the indiscipline of some NPFL fighters diverted their attention to looting rather than completing the attack on Monrovia. ECOMOG fought alongside AFL and ULIMO units in open alliance. In general, AFL and ULIMO units would form the front lines of attack while ECOMOG supported their operations with heavy weapons. The undisciplined AFL and ULIMO soldiers were responsible for significant brutality and looting in the campaign to repulse the NPFL.[49]

As ECOMOG increased its attacks on the NPFL, criticisms and divisions within West Africa grew.[50] U.S. Assistant Secretary of State for African Affairs Herman Cohen stated that "ECOWAS is no longer a neutral party."[51] Nigeria, however, increased its troop strength and began a long and bloody offensive (supporting by aerial bombardment and strafing by ECOMOG jets) that forced Taylor back toward Gbarnga. Human rights groups criticized ECOMOG and noted that while the intervention "succeeded in temporarily stopping the bloodshed and ethnic killing . . . pursuing peace without recognizing the centrality of human rights has left ECOMOG embroiled in a conflict with few immediate prospects for resolution."[52]

ECOMOG's 12,000-man force denied Taylor victory but had greater difficulty in imposing a long-term political solution. ECOMOG seemingly could not link its use of military force to a diplomatic agenda to generate movement toward a political solution. The large-scale destruction caused new splits within West Africa and new factions to develop among Liberians, greatly complicating the peacemaking process. ECOWAS leaders, particularly Burkina Faso and Côte d'Ivoire, became increasingly exasperated and critical. Benin's President Nicéphore Soglo was reported by the American embassy to have "thrown up his hands over Liberia, deciding that Nigeria has taken over ECOMOG and that ECOWAS is too divided to have a common policy for a peaceful resolution of the problem. 'Let them fight,' he mutters often, 'until they are exhausted.'"[53]

In November 1992, in the aftermath of Operation Octopus, ECOWAS imposed sanctions against Taylor, and the United Nations imposed an arms embargo against Liberia.[54] In addition, the secretary general added a new set of actors to this increasingly complicated mix by appointing a UN special representative, the Jamaican Trevor

Gordon-Somers, to coordinate the UN's activities and encourage a mediated settlement.

The diplomatic efforts to find a negotiated solution to the Liberian crisis were undermined in part by divisions within West Africa. A number of West African states, most notably Burkina Faso and Côte d'Ivoire, provided assistance and freedom of movement to Charles Taylor. Sierra Leone and Guinea, in turn, supported Taylor's rivals in ULIMO. These regional alliances allowed various factions to create trading networks where they sold diamonds, timber, rubber, and goods looted during the fighting in exchange for weapons and other matériel to sustain their fighting forces.[55] ECOMOG forces themselves engaged in and protected this lucrative trade.[56] A number of international private firms also traded with various factional leaders, providing additional resources to the war.[57] The imposition of ECOWAS and UN sanctions created obstacles to some of this trade but never cut off the vital links that allowed the fighting to continue.

In 1993 Taylor began to lose ground to the combined forces of ECOMOG and ULIMO. ECOMOG, in an effort to prevent violations of its sanctions, seized the port of Buchanan, further restricting Taylor's access to markets.[58] ECOMOG doubted that Taylor would ever agree to a negotiated settlement and began to concentrate on defeating him militarily. ECOMOG and Nigerian leaders in particular believed that the military balance had shifted in their favor and that they would soon oust Taylor from his Gbarnga base.[59] ECOMOG's massive use of force, including aerial bombardment and shelling from Nigerian gunboats that destroyed large parts of the port city of Greenville and a controversial attack on the Phebe Hospital near Gbarnga, forced Taylor to pull back.[60]

At the very moment that the major factional leaders seemed weakest, talks to establish a political framework raised their stature once again and made them the focus of peace efforts. UN-sponsored meetings in Geneva led to a further set of talks and an agreement signed in Cotonou, Benin, in July 1993. This relatively comprehensive agreement was signed by IGNU, ULIMO, and NPFL. Recent ECOMOG attacks encouraged Taylor to accept the cease-fire, although his commitment to implementation remained suspect. Sawyer's interim government was replaced by the Liberian National Transitional Government (LNTG), a collective government headed by a five-member Council of State nominated by NPFL, ULIMO, and IGNU. To a significant extent the Cotonou Agreement represented an abandoning of efforts to build a viable interim civilian government. Rather than press its military campaign against Taylor, ECOWAS offered him a political settlement. Future interim governments would be dominated by representatives appointed by the warring factions. As with earlier agreements, the Cotonou Agreement called for encampment of warring factions and elections after a seven-month period of transitional rule.[61]

To overcome previous failures in implementation and to appease Taylor's criticisms of Nigeria's role, the Cotonou Agreement called for an expansion of ECOMOG to include contingents from outside the region. ECOMOG was made less Nigerian-dominated by the addition of some 1,500 troops from Tanzania and Uganda, a step intended to reassure Taylor, who refused to disarm to ECOMOG. Delays in deployment and lack of resources, however, limited participation (Zimbabwe declined to participate because of financial problems), and murky command and control further hampered the expanded force. Lack of logistical capacity and poor communications continued to bedevil ECOMOG. Besides expanding the number of contingents in ECOMOG in order to address questions of Nigerian neutrality, the agreement assigned responsibility for supervision and monitoring of the implementation process jointly to ECOMOG and the United Nations. In response, the UN established a small but symbolic UN Observer Mission in Liberia (UNOMIL) in September 1993.[62] The operation included lightly armed peacekeepers without the capability or mandate to join ECOMOG in its peace enforcement activities.

UNOMIL represented a new approach for the United Nations in dealing with peacekeeping. Driven by West Africa's (and especially Nigeria's) desire to maintain control over the operation and the general reluctance by the United Nations to take on more peacekeeping or peace enforcement operations, UNOMIL's mandate was developed as a chapter VIII operation. Under chapter VIII of the UN Charter, the Security Council may authorize a regional organization to undertake peace enforcement operations. Under resolution 866, the United Nations established UNOMIL to closely mirror ECOMOG.

> Since the role foreseen for UNOMIL is to monitor and verify the implementation of the [Cotonou] Agreement, its concept of operation necessarily must be parallel to that of ECOMOG. . . . UNOMIL would thus . . . deploy observer teams in concert with ECOMOG

deployment. . . . UNOMIL and ECOMOG would collaborate closely in their operations."[63]

UNOMIL would thus facilitate the implementation of the Cotonou Agreement by monitoring the military aspects (cease-fire, disarmament, demobilization, and the arms embargo) and verifying their impartial application. In addition, civilian components would work on electoral assistance and coordinate humanitarian operations. UNOMIL had several hundred military observers in 1994 and 1995, but these were lightly armed peacekeepers, and deployment outside of ECOMOG-protected areas in Monrovia was sporadic.[64] In addition, UNOMIL remained underfunded as the international community devoted its attention to higher profile peace operations in Bosnia, Haiti, and Angola.

After a series of squabbles and delays over the composition of the new cabinet, the Liberian National Transitional Government (LNTG) was finally sworn in on March 7, 1994, under the chairmanship of David Kpomakpor, a lawyer and academic.[65] These delays threw implementation off schedule from the start. In addition, disarmament never developed momentum and the Ugandan and Tanzanian forces attached to ECOMOG soon came under attack by the NPFL, recognized that there was no peace to keep, and withdrew.[66] By mid-1994, it was clear that the Cotonou Agreement was inoperative, and elections once scheduled for September 1994 had to be canceled.

The conflict became complicated further with the creation of a new set of factions. The Liberian Peace Council (LPC, drawn from Krahn elements in the AFL and ULIMO), challenged the NPFL in Grand Gedeh County (the Krahn home territory) in eastern Liberia while the Lofa Defense Force developed in Lofa County in retaliation against abuses by ULIMO.[67] Some analysts suggest that these new forces were designed as proxies to continue the fighting while allowing the signatories to the peace agreement to claim they had no authority over the new groups. Nigeria reportedly favored the various Krahn groups in the AFL, LPC, and ULIMO, regarding them as allies in the war against the NPFL and as potential rulers once the NPFL was finished and ECOMOG could withdraw.[68] Besides these new factions, the ever present tensions and competition for leadership between the Krahn and the Mandingo wings of ULIMO broke out into open warfare in 1994.[69] The Krahn faction was led by Roosevelt Johnson and was known as ULIMO-J while the Mandingo faction was led by Alhaji Kromah and was known as ULIMO-K.

Furthermore tensions within the NPFL erupted in July 1994 as a dissident faction tried to take over the movement and violence erupted around Gbarnga. A group known as the NPFL-Central Revolutionary Council (CRC-NPFL), led by senior NPFL officials Sam Dokie and Tom Woewiyu, claimed to have removed Taylor from leadership. For a period, the CRC-NPFL controlled Gbarnga, working in collaboration with ULIMO, LPC, and AFL. New waves of fighting and displacement erupted while the formation of the transitional government stalled and disarmament faltered. UN observers and humanitarian workers again were taken hostage by various factions in September 1994.[70]

Finally, a bizarre coup attempt by Charles Julu in September 1994 further increased the sense that events in Liberia were out of control. Julu was a former AFL general responsible for carrying out Doe's scorched earth campaign in Nimba County in retaliation for Taylor's 1989 invasion. He and one hundred supporters briefly occupied the Executive Mansion in Monrovia before being bombed out of the building by ECOMOG gunboats.[71] Rather than moving toward a coherent and peaceful transitional process, Liberia seemed to be shattering into violent pieces and spreading disorder to its neighbors while international peacekeepers retreated to the safety of Monrovia.[72]

A new series of negotiations (Akosombo, Ghana, in September 1994, and Accra, Ghana, in November 1994 and January 1995) led by Ghana's president and new ECOWAS chair, Jerry Rawlings, resulted in the creation of a new Council of State with seats reserved for the various factional leaders (including the new factions that had arisen since the seats were last divided among factions in Cotonou). Elections were scheduled again, this time for October 1995. The Akosombo Agreement dissolved the existing transitional government and replaced it with nominees of the three factions who participated in the talks. Many regarded this as again rescuing the militia leaders when their power was eroding and the transitional government demonstrating some autonomy.[73] In a clear indication of the increasingly multilateral nature of the conflict and the dominance of military factions in the peace talks by late 1994, no fewer than eight groups (seven of them armed factions) signed the agreement in Accra. The three signatories of the Akosombo Agreement, the NPFL, ULIMO-K, and AFL, were joined by ULIMO-J, the Lofa Defense Force, LPC, CRC-NPFL, and the civilian Liberia National Conference.

The Abuja Peace Process

Arguments over the composition and membership of the latest Council of State got nowhere until a meeting took place between Taylor and the new Nigerian head of state, Sani Abacha, in June 1995.[74] Abacha had just replaced Rawlings as chair of ECOWAS and made solving the Liberian crisis a test of his regional leadership. Rumors about a secret deal between Abacha and Taylor abounded among Liberian observers. Nigeria seemed to have revised its position from attempting to defeat Taylor to accepting that his accession to power was inevitable. After more than five years of fighting and immeasurable destruction, Nigeria was prepared to accept what it had intervened to prevent. The main question remaining was what mechanism would achieve that goal while allowing ECOWAS and Nigeria to receive the credit for a successful mission.

Under pressure from an increasingly impatient ECOWAS, a new agreement was signed among the warring factions in Abuja, Nigeria, on August 19, 1995.[75] Under the Abuja Accord, a revamped, six-member Council of State was installed on September 1, which included leaders of the ruling factions and three civilians. Wilton Sankawulo, an academic without political experience, became chair of the new Council. According to one analyst, "Abuja basically offered the warlords the spoils of office in a desperate attempt to buy peace by giving them a stake in keeping it."[76] Following the agreement, Taylor and some of his troops entered Monrovia to join the new government. Some diplomats and observers regarded Taylor's embrace of the Abuja Accord as an important sign that this agreement would hold.[77]

The Abuja Accord called for disarmament by January 1996 and elections by August 1996, a very rapid timetable. As with previous efforts, however, the combination of factional leaders maneuvering for advantage and the slow pace at which the United Nations and ECOMOG put programs in place made such deadlines unreachable.[78] Implementation stalled, disarmament fell behind schedule, ECOMOG could not deploy throughout the country, refugees could not return home, and nongovernmental organizations continued to face threats to their humanitarian work.

Violations of the cease-fire continued. Roosevelt Johnson and ULIMO-J defected from the agreement and attacked ECOMOG peace-keepers near Tubmanburg in December 1995, inflicting nearly one hundred casualties and capturing large amounts of military equipment.[79] Many have suggested that the fighting was motivated in part by a dispute between Johnson and Nigerian peacekeepers over control of diamond and gold mines in the area.[80] Some believed that the militia leaders did not want an end to the situation that allowed them to make lucrative deals on the black market.[81] ECOMOG began operations to isolate Johnson and supported the efforts by Taylor and Kromah to marginalize their rival.[82]

April 6, 1996

Violence reached new heights when another round of vicious urban fighting erupted in Monrovia in April 1996. Taylor and his ally of the moment, Kromah, dismissed Johnson from the interim government and moved against his largely Krahn militia.[83] Taylor may have underestimated the fighting capacity of the members of Johnson's small but well-trained and well-armed force (drawn from ULIMO-J, AFL, and LPC), which was holed up at the Barclay Training Center compound in downtown Monrovia and had their backs against the wall.[84] The ensuing battle "collapsed into a murderous farce" that destroyed the city and ended hopes that Liberia could hold an election any time soon.[85] According to the United Nations, "It can safely be stated that all humanitarian organizations, United Nations agencies, non-governmental organizations, UNOMIL, and government offices, as well as shops and other commercial establishments, were systematically looted by fighters of all factions."[86] ECOMOG seemed powerless or unwilling to contain the fighting (some have alleged that elements of ECOMOG cooperated with the looting).[87]

The factions targeted many of the nascent institutions of civil society. The Justice and Peace Commission of the National Catholic Secretariat, for example, was hit and all its documents, equipment, and only vehicle looted or destroyed. Its leader, Samuel Kofi Woods for a time fled the country for his life.[88] Newspaper and independent radio offices were burned down and most international relief officials fled after being looted and threatened. According to former IGNU leader Amos Sawyer, "The big three warlords . . . have decided they are going to crush whatever civilian opposition they can. Whatever they had not succeeded in bullying out of existence or shutting down through rigged courts they have just crushed."[89]

By early May 1996, it looked as if Taylor had miscalculated as his erstwhile ally Kromah left Monrovia, Johnson's men remained dug in at Barclay's Training Center, and new groups of Krahn fighters entered the city and attacked Taylor's stronghold in Congo Town. West African leaders organized a new round of talks in Accra, Ghana, in an effort to end the fighting and to reestablish the transitional government. The Accra meeting established a new cease-fire and restored Johnson to his cabinet position. Pressure to accept a new cease-fire came from the threat by ECOMOG to withdraw from Liberia.[90] By June, ECOMOG had reestablished some semblance of security in Monrovia but not before nearly everything of value in the city had been looted or destroyed.

CONCLUSION

The Liberian civil war in 1996 was a stalemate between Charles Taylor's National Patriotic Front for Liberia (NPFL) and the Nigerian-led Economic Community of West African States Cease-Fire Monitoring Group (ECOMOG). The other Liberian factions made advances or held territory by moving into vacuums created by NPFL and ECOMOG moves. The NPFL remained convinced that it alone had the power and the right to run the country and had the capacity to continue to pursue its objectives through unilateral military moves if the transitional process threatened to weaken its position. ECOMOG had demonstrated an ability to prevent Taylor from winning the civil war but no capacity to build an alternative political structure to contain him, and the broader international community had made it clear through the seven years of conflict that it was not interested in initiating a dangerous and expensive peace enforcement mission in Liberia.

The Yamoussoukro, Cotonou, Akosombo, Accra, and the first Abuja Accords all failed in part because each created a transitional process that lacked the support of an armed faction capable of derailing implementation. Continued fighting by ULIMO and LPC before they were incorporated into the agreements made adherence to the ambitious timetables impossible. The NPFL often signed agreements to gain time to regroup and to pursue its objectives through unilateral military action. ECOMOG failed to implement the agreements adequately because of a lack of resources (particularly transportation) and because it relied upon local allies (AFL, ULIMO) to help contain the NPFL, making the NPFL reluctant to disarm to an organization it regarded as a partisan enemy. The international community limited its support both because it doubted the sincerity of the warring factions' commitment to peace and distrusted Nigeria's motives.

The interim institutions set up by the various peace agreements failed to include the full range of actors necessary to sustain the transition and furthermore lacked mechanisms to engage the factions in ongoing talks and joint decisionmaking that may have built confidence in the process. Instead, the early interim government was dominated by civilian groups and was regarded by one of the key parties, the NPFL, as an opponent. Later the interim governments were composed of councils divided among competing factional leaders. These factionally divided interim governments failed in part because new factions continuously rose up to demand their seat at the table (and share of the spoils) and because the councils lacked institutional mechanisms to generate consensus among the polarized groups. Without an effective interim regime, the transitions envisioned in each of the peace agreements failed to generate adequate support.

In addition, the fundamental issues relating to distribution of power and the absence of institutions to check personal rule that lay at the source of the political violence in Liberia since the 1970s remained unexamined. Rather than recognizing that the state that collapsed in Liberia in 1990 broke down in part because of the concentration of power in the presidency and a constitutional order that lacked effective checks and balances, the regional peace process focused on whether Taylor should be allowed to assume the presidency. On occasion during the conflict, civic groups and human rights organizations raised the issue of the need to reform government institutions and the constitution to avoid another crisis such as 1990.[91] In general, however, neither the factional leaders nor the regional states looked beyond the question of who would rule. By 1996 and 1997, a number of Liberians, given the horrors of the war, understandably remembered the Doe regime as "normal times" and wished to return to such an order, failing to recall how the structures of power that Doe created and exploited led to brutal personal rule and violent resistance.

The experiment in regional peace enforcement represented by ECOMOG had failed to find a workable formula that combined the use of force with a political strategy by 1996. The operation had been expensive, both in terms of financial resources and casualties, shouldered largely by Nigeria. One scholar estimates that as many as 700 West African soldiers died in combat during the intervention.[92] Nigerian head of state General Sani Abacha claimed that his country had spent more than $3 billion in support of ECOMOG activities in Liberia.[93] Regardless of the actual figures, ECOMOG represented the most prominent example of peace enforcement by a regional organization in Africa.

The fundamental difficulties in managing internal conflicts and the mixed record of UN peace enforcement suggest that such disappointing results are not surprising.[94] ECOMOG suffered from the same perils that have plagued peace-enforcement operations elsewhere, "an intractable local situation and a lack of genuine consensus at the international level."[95] The reasoning behind the intervention, however, was suspect from the start because the conflict had not reached a stalemate before the intervention and ECOMOG was never regarded as a neutral peacekeeper. By mid-1996, ECOMOG had transformed a war that probably would have ended in a quick victory for Taylor into a protracted struggle, increased casualties, caused a splintering of political movements making conflict management more difficult, and an expansion of the conflict into neighboring Sierra Leone.[96]

3
THE JULY 19, 1997, SPECIAL ELECTIONS

The collapse into another spasm of murderous anarchy in April 1996 forced Liberia's neighbors to reassess their policy toward the conflict.[1] West African foreign ministers from the ECOWAS Committee of Nine mandated to manage the intervention met for a new round of talks in Abuja, Nigeria, in August 1996. The major factional leaders—Charles Taylor, Alhaji Kromah, George Boley, and Roosevelt Johnson—all attended and signed a revised agreement. The Abuja II Accord reaffirmed the Abuja I framework but extended the timetable for implementation by nine months and threatened sanctions, including a prohibition against running for elective office, against any leader who violated the agreement. Under Abuja II, disarmament was to begin in November 1996 and elections were scheduled for May 1997. According to one Western diplomat, "Sani Abacha wants to get out of Liberia. To do that, he has to find a workable end-game strategy, which will have to involve elections."[2] Following the Abuja meetings, a cease-fire was declared on August 20, 1996, and Ruth Perry (Africa's first female head of state) replaced Wilton Sankawulo as the chair of the Liberian Council of State.[3]

The Abuja II agreement represented a final effort to accommodate the contending forces and to create a context to transform the cycle of failed interim regimes, violations of cease-fires, ineffective disarmament, and continued clashes between ECOMOG and various factions. The highest priority of the ECOWAS foreign ministers who proposed the Abuja Accord was to end the war. Other goals, ranging from democratization, promotion of the rule of law, reforming the military, repatriating refugees, and reestablishing state services such as schools and health programs, were all predicated on ending the conflict and constructing some form of stability. Under the Abuja Accord, as with earlier agreements, an election was the chosen mechanism for accomplishing that critical goal.

IMPLEMENTING THE ABUJA II ACCORD

Several important changes marked the final peace agreement. ECOMOG increased its forces in anticipation of its critical role in implementing the Abuja Accord. Under the assertive leadership of Nigerian Major General Victor Malu, the force expanded to 12,000 troops, including contingents from Côte d'Ivoire and Burkina Faso (states that previously had opposed ECOMOG and supported Taylor).[4] In addition, Côte d'Ivoire began to crack down on the cross-border trade that had sustained Taylor throughout the war.[5] The old splits within West Africa that had weakened ECOMOG since its creation were overcome for a period by the sense of urgency to end the conflict.

Malu was a dynamic and forceful commander whom the Liberian press referred to without irony as the "strongman of Liberia." After the failures of earlier ECOMOG commanders, Malu earned the respect of a large number of Liberians for his no-nonsense commitment to maintain order. The new leader built confidence within Liberia by using a firm hand to contain any forces that challenged ECOMOG's authority and by demonstrating a keen aptitude for managing his public image. Human rights groups, however, alleged that ECOMOG severely beat prisoners and used undue force.[6] ECOMOG seemed determined not to let the factions gain the initiative on the ground again as they had during the April 1996 fighting and looting. When a minor skirmish broke out in Monrovia on August 10, for example, ECOMOG quickly deployed well-armed troops to every major intersection and aggressively patrolled the streets in tanks and armored personnel carriers.[7] Signs reading "Thank God for ECOMOG" covered the walls of bombed-out buildings across Monrovia.

During late 1996, numerous cease-fire violations threatened to derail the Abuja process. As with earlier agreements, it seemed as if the factions had signed for tactical reasons and continued to jockey for strategic positions and control over economic assets. In September 1996, another massacre took place in Sinje, Grand Cape Mount County, when a number of civilians were killed during a raid to steal recently delivered food relief supplies. In October, the NPFL took control of the strategic port city of Greenville, gaining a key logging center and displacing the Liberia Peace Council from its main base of operations.[8] On October 31, 1996, gunmen opened fire in the Executive Mansion in Monrovia in an alleged attempt to assassinate Taylor.[9] Despite the evidence that factions were violating the Abuja Agreements, ECOWAS decided not to invoke sanctions for fear that the party singled out for punishment would withdraw from the peace process, compelling ECOMOG to return to peace enforcement.

ECOMOG eventually deployed its troops to forty-eight locations in every Liberian county.[10] Regular patrols and checkpoints protected the main roads and facilitated the movement of humanitarian shipments. The sight of drugged child soldiers manning road blocks and extorting money and resources from nongovernmental organizations and any other unarmed traveler, a regular characteristic of the previous seven years, virtually disappeared. One of the few advantages Liberia had over similar postconflict transitions in Cambodia, Angola, and Mozambique was the general absence of land mines.

The U.S., German, and Dutch governments provided needed logistical support to ECOMOG, particularly in the form of communications equipment, trucks, helicopters, and logistics maintenance. The U.S.-based firm of Pacific Architects and Engineers (PAE) received funding from the United States to keep ECOMOG vehicles on the road and leased helicopters flying, thereby giving ECOMOG the ability to respond quickly for the first time.[11] In addition, the United States and the United Kingdom provided military airlifts for additional troops to join ECOMOG from Ghana, Mali, and Côte d'Ivoire. Nigerians continued to form the bulk of the force but other contingents, notably those from Ghana and Benin, performed their tasks professionally and made important contributions.

Observers differed in their interpretations of the increased security within Liberia in 1997. While ECOMOG had better leadership and a far superior ability to move quickly thanks to the assistance provided by PAE, many doubted that it could sustain a systematic series of attacks in the countryside or handle large crowds or riots within

Monrovia.[12] In any event, security incidents were few and relatively easy to manage by early 1997, in part because of ECOMOG's increased capacity and in part because the leaders of the factions chose not to explore military options during this period. In the end, ECOMOG and the strongest faction, the NPFL, had a common interest in maintaining security because both believed the election would suit their interests.

Conditions in 1997

Although disarmament began slowly in November 1996, the process picked up momentum toward the end of January 1997, and the deadline for handing in weapons was extended for ten days until February 9. ECOMOG collected large quantities of weapons and for the first time in years guns were not visible on the streets except in the hands of the peacekeepers. Factional roadblocks became rare in most areas. ECOMOG checkpoints regularly searched vehicles for weapons and conducted a series of cordon and search operations across Monrovia. According to official figures, 21,315 fighters (including 4,306 children) were disarmed, and some 10,000 weapons recovered.[13] Malu enjoyed taking prominent visitors such as former U.S. President Jimmy Carter on tours of the containers filled with seized weapons stored at ECOMOG bases in Monrovia. Throughout the spring, ECOMOG regularly announced that it had found new arms caches in the areas formerly under the control of each of the factions. In March 1997, ECOMOG briefly detained Alhaji Kromah, the head of ULIMO-K, after large quantities of heavy weapons were discovered in his Monrovia home.[14]

While many arms were collected, demobilization in terms of breaking the command and control structures over fighters was far less complete. Demobilization remained a difficult problem to manage, owing in part to the nature of the fighting forces in Liberia and the large numbers of "casual fighters" and child soldiers.[15] Scarce resources and poor planning reduced demobilization to a twelve-hour process whereby ex-combatants simply turned in a weapon (or even a handful of bullets), received a registration card, and then were left on their own. According to one report, the level of planning for disarmament, demobilization, and reintegration was "frighteningly inadequate."[16] Victor Tanner concludes that, although Abuja II did more than any other peace agreement regarding disarmament and demobilization, the exercise was in many regards "hollow."[17] Many of the weapons turned in were not serviceable, and few doubted that the most reliable fighters avoided demobilization while the young and inexperienced went through the process in the hope of obtaining social services or other benefits.

The United Nations Development Program and the U.S. Agency for International Development (USAID) created some programs to engage ex-combatants in public works such as road repair and ditch clearance, but these were not long-term employment programs, and few social reintegration packages were developed. Unlike other demobilization programs, no "decompression" period to promote the reintegration of former combatants into civilian life was instituted. Groups of young unemployed ex-combatants continued to congregate on street corners ready to be remobilized rapidly. Furthermore, some quick jobs programs hired entire units intact, including commanders, thereby sustaining the old factional command and control structures. In any event, these programs were discontinued after the July elections, leaving unemployed fighters to search for work as best they could.

By early 1997, increased stability had provided Liberians with an opportunity to begin rebuilding their lives. By March, Monrovia's streets had come alive with small traders, a large market of used clothing (and looted office equipment), and chop houses selling food and drinks. Large numbers remained in refugee camps, but assessment teams noted that some men were traveling from the camps to survey their old villages in preparation for return. Although a few did repatriate, most planned to wait until after the election to see if peace endured. In addition, the international community provided better services in food, medical care, and education in the camps than in Liberia.[18] The same pattern held true in the huge camps of internally displaced persons that surrounded Monrovia. Most displaced persons indicated that they wanted to return home, but they worried about this latest peace agreement holding. They needed assistance in the form of transportation and food and materials to sustain them while they rebuilt their homes destroyed during the war. In addition, the office of the United Nations High Commissioner for Refugees and other international organizations, remembering the chaos of April 1996, were reluctant to encourage repatriation until security was more firmly established.

Economic activity in early 1997 was based almost exclusively on humanitarian relief and employment by international organizations and NGOs. Agricultural production was minimal and basic social services such as education and health care were virtually nonexistent. Monrovia lacked electrical power, piped water, and mail service, and made do with a very patchy phone system. International NGOs relied upon generators, radio communications, and couriers. Government ministries often lacked working phones, office equipment, or the funds to pay employees. The interim Council of State was led by Ruth Perry, who demonstrated her interest in social issues and rehabilitation through a series of trips to the war-torn countryside. The factional composition of the Council and its almost complete lack of resources, however, made it unable to implement programs or govern effectively. The country, in desperate need of basic social services, drifted while ECOMOG provided security and international NGOs and UN agencies provided basic humanitarian relief. Although conditions were better than any time since 1990, new institutions were needed to make it sustainable.

Political Actors during the Transition

On February 28, 1997, factional leaders who wished to run for office resigned from the Council of State as required in the Abuja Accord. Although the leaders stepped down, each handpicked his successor on the Council, ensuring that factional control (and hence deadlock) persisted. Several converted their militias into political parties. Charles Taylor transformed his NPFL into the National Patriotic Party (NPP), Alhaji Kromah turned his ULIMO-K into the All Liberian Coalition Party (ALCOP), and LPC leader George Boley eventually became the standard-bearer for the late President Doe's former party, the National Democratic Party of Liberia (NDPL). Roosevelt Johnson, the ULIMO-J leader who was at the center of the April 1996 fighting, announced that he would not seek elective office.

In addition to these former factions, a number of previously established political parties began organizing for the upcoming campaign. Several civilian political leaders, many from the generation that initiated the demonstrations of the late 1970s that sparked the overthrow of William Tolbert and the True Whig regime and who were involved in the 1985 elections, were anxious to run and demonstrate that they—not the former factional leaders—represented the peaceful aspirations of the majority of Liberians. In January 1997 the major civilian politicians founded the Alliance of Political Parties and promised to work together to provide Liberian voters a clear alternative to the former factional leaders.[19] The alliance held a contentious convention in March and nominated Cletus Wortoson of the Liberian Action Party (LAP) as its presidential candidate. Personal ambitions and allegations of vote buying and other irregularities, however, led several prominent politicians, including Togba-Nah Tipoteh (Liberia People's Party) and Baccus Matthews (United People's Party), to withdraw. The Unity Party also left the alliance and nominated Ellen Johnson Sirleaf as its candidate. Sirleaf formerly was one of the original leaders of LAP in the 1980s, served as a senator, was arrested by Doe, and later served as an official with the United Nations Development Program in New York.

Thirteen candidates for president and their associated slates for the Senate and House of Representatives qualified for the ballot.[20] Sirleaf and the Unity Party quickly appeared to be the leading contender to challenge Taylor and his National Patriotic Party. The Alliance of Political Parties crumbled, and major civilian leaders began to gravitate toward Sirleaf. The other parties were either regionally or ethnically identified (ALCOP never fully overcame its image as a Mandingo party and NDPL had a strong Krahn identity) or small civilian parties with only a limited capacity to campaign in the countryside. The Unity Party seemed positioned to appeal to Liberians who wanted a candidate not associated with the recent violence.

Taylor's NPP, however, had an enormous financial and organizational advantage, building on the structures developed during the war and the resources controlled as a result of the conflict.[21] Taylor had a countrywide institutional infrastructure that had a presence in nearly every village and the resources to distribute rice to displaced camps and to run a wide-ranging humanitarian operation. Taylor also maintained control over the government's shortwave radio station, the only media accessible to large areas of the countryside for years leading up to the election. The NPP campaign suggested to voters who had no access to neutral information that Taylor was already president and the election was designed merely to ratify his power.

The Electoral System and Timetable

Following a United Nations technical survey mission in December 1996, ECOWAS and the United Nations called for a Special Election Package that would provide the framework for what was explicitly an extraconstitutional election.[22] In February, ECOWAS decided that as a result of the massive displacement during the civil war, the old system of single-member majoritarian constituencies was impossible for the 1997 Special Elections.[23] It therefore proposed a proportional system with a single national constituency for the legislature while maintaining a majoritarian presidency. This decision allowed Liberia to defer the difficult process of conducting a census and redistricting, but it was never understood by many Liberians.

Despite the challenges of conducting the election in an environment disrupted by conflict, ECOWAS and international technical advisers tried to design an electoral system that resembled the prewar pattern and the Liberian Constitution as closely as possible. The new government would have a president and vice president elected on a single ticket. In the event that no presidential candidate won a majority of the votes, a runoff would be held. As before, legislative authority would be vested in a Congress composed of a House of Representatives and a Senate. The House of Representatives would include sixty-four members and the Senate would consist of twenty-six seats, two for each of the thirteen counties. As noted, the legislature would be selected on the basis of proportional representation in a single, nationwide constituency. Liberians across the political spectrum supported the decision to model the new government on the institutions included in the 1986 Constitution but remained unclear about the precise implications of the proportional representation system.

Several scholars have argued that proportional representation is a more effective electoral system in postconflict or ethnically divided countries because it encourages inclusion and coalition government. Majoritarian systems, in contrast, are more likely to limit representation from minority groups.[24] The Liberian system represented a hybrid of the two types, with the president elected in a majoritarian system holding most of the power under the old Liberian constitution. Given the nature of the peace process, the powerful presidency created by the pre-war Liberian constitution, and the imbalances of power, the inclusionary aspects derived from the proportional system for the parliament played only a very minor role.

In addition to determining the electoral system, ECOWAS decided that the estimated 800,000 Liberians in refugee camps, primarily in Guinea and Côte d'Ivoire, would have to return to Liberia in order to vote.[25] The United Nations earlier had recommended a system that would have permitted refugees to vote in their camps, but the neighboring states vetoed the idea. This decision was widely supported within Liberia where fears of manipulation made most citizens wary of people voting outside the country. The lack of resources and infrastructure in Liberia, however, limited the number of refugees who could return to vote and thereby effectively disenfranchised a large segment of the population.[26] UNHCR developed an eighteen-month repatriation plan, providing few resources for refugees interested in returning in time to vote.

The Abuja II Accord called for a new elections commission to manage the electoral process. The Independent Elections Commission (IECOM) finally was inducted on April 2, nearly a month behind schedule.[27] It consisted of three members nominated by the three main factions (NPFL, ULIMO-K, LPC), and one each selected by women, youth, unions, and civilian political parties. It was chaired by G. Henry Andrews, a former journalist who was nominated by the civilian parties.[28] The selection of the women's and youth representatives engendered considerable controversy as Taylor's allies objected to the proposed members. In addition, ECOWAS, the Organization of African Unity, and the United Nations each named a nonvoting international commissioner. The commission represented as broad a range of Liberian political interests as any organization in the country at the time, but lack of time and resources combined with inexperience hindered its work. Furthermore, IECOM had difficulty establishing its autonomy from ECOWAS and lacked the mandate to make decisions on matters such as the electoral timetable established in the Abuja Accord. From the start, many doubted IECOM's capacity to organize elections by the May 30, 1997, deadline.

Although the broad components of the electoral system to be used in the Special Election had been announced, critical details were lacking. Political parties did not know the rules relating to deadlines for party registration, the criteria for party candidate lists, and many other legal requirements that affected their campaigns. The process of debating and drafting the Special Elections Law took place largely between IECOM and ECOWAS and did not involve Liberian political parties or civic organizations in a serious or systematic manner. As with so many aspects of the peace process dating back to 1990, regional leaders and the factions drove the process while civilians remained on the margins.

Even the question of the term of office of the government chosen in the Special Election remained unclear during April and May. Some suggested a term shorter than the six years provided for in the prewar constitution, but little public discussion took place. Other issues that had been hotly debated in other states undergoing similar transitions remained largely unmentioned. Postelection powersharing or the need to negotiate the composition of the new Armed Forces of Liberia, for example, received little attention. The Carter Center tried to engage political leaders in a discussion of postelection governance issues without success. Charles Taylor in particular objected to any process that might limit his powers following the electoral victory he anticipated. Key Nigerian policymakers also favored a strong, unified government to contain disorder. Political leaders generally preferred to allow the election to settle such contentious issues. Other Liberians worried that a powersharing pact and broad-based government might result in another weak regime like the series of flawed interim governments that they had suffered under since 1990.

Soon after induction, IECOM signaled that it could not meet the May 30, 1997, deadline for elections as called for in Abuja II. The inability or unwillingness of the Council of State to provide funds for IECOM to cover salaries continually stalled the process. Rivalry and misunderstandings between international donors and ECOWAS complicated assistance. On April 23, IECOM suspended the deadlines for party conventions, party lists, and the start of the thirty-day campaign period, signaling that a postponement was inevitable.[29] ECOWAS Special Envoy and Nigerian Foreign Minister Chief Tom Ikimi led an assessment team to Monrovia from April 24 to April 27 and met with political parties and IECOM to assess preparations. The IECOM and most political parties (but not Taylor's NPP) asked ECOWAS to consider an extension of the electoral schedule. Ikimi, however, stated that the decision rested with ECOWAS, not Liberians, and "only the ECOWAS heads of state can take a decision."[30] The UN secretary general wrote to ECOWAS chairman Sani Abacha and expressed his concerns that the election timetable was too tight and that a joint coordination mechanism—not unilateral ECOWAS proclamations—was needed to take decisions under the chapter VIII peacekeeping mandate.[31] International donors indicated that they could not support the process financially until the legal framework for the election was finalized and made public.

An increasing number of Liberian civic and political groups began to speak out on the need for credible elections, and many urged a postponement. An Inter-Party Working Group of eleven registered political parties (that again did not include Taylor's NPP) signed a statement on May 1 that listed a variety of preconditions ranging from disarmament and demobilization, repatriation and resettlement, access to the countryside, an independent elections commission, and the creation of a level playing field. The statement concluded with a demand "that the date for the holding of election[s] be rescheduled bearing in mind the need to satisfy the conditions stated herein before the elections are held; such a new date for elections shall however not be before the second Tuesday of October, 1997."[32] This statement seemed to suggest that key Liberian actors with a stake in the forthcoming elections were concerned that conditions did not favor their cause and were organizing to insist that their voice be heard in the deliberations on the election system.

Taylor's NPP and ECOWAS, however, continued to keep up the pressure for adhering to the May 30 deadline stipulated in the Abuja Accord. Taylor warned that he would not feel bound by any of the Abuja provisions if the election date was changed. Several ECOMOG troop-contributing states, notably Ghana, threatened to withdraw their forces immediately if the elections were postponed. These powerful pressures on IECOM made planning and thoughtful consideration of the requirements of a credible electoral process difficult.

The debate over the timing of the Liberian election revolved around whether May 30 or some date during the summer or at the latest October was the most appropriate. Most criticisms related largely to the technical requirements of registration and access to the countryside during the rainy season. Although many urged a delay of several months, few argued for a longer transition of several years to allow for repatriation of refugees, effective demobilization of combatants, and a rebuilding of secure communities. ECOWAS made it clear that it would never accept such a lengthy transition and the broader international community had demonstrated a clear lack of interest in Liberia over the previous seven years. The interim Council of State was not functional, and Liberia lacked even basic government services. Seven years of ineffective interim governments led many Liberians to oppose any plan to create a longer transitional government. The structures established by ECOMOG and the Abuja Accord could not hold for long and a rapid conclusion to the transition, either through an election or another political breakdown and resurgence of violence, seemed unavoidable.

The political parties finally were invited to an Extraordinary Summit Meeting of the ECOWAS Committee of Nine in Abuja for consultations on the Special Elections Package on May 16, 1997.[33] After meeting with ECOWAS chairman Sani Abacha, the parties, despite their earlier public demand for a postponement until October, accepted a decision to postpone until July 19.[34] The IECOM told the parties that it could provide a copy of the Special Law for review, complete registration, and conduct voters' education within this timetable. The political parties accepted these promises. In addition, they pushed to have a single ballot, which they argued was more appropriate for proportional representation and counting at the polling sites, rather than the two ballots (one for the majoritarian presidential election and one for the proportional legislative election) and centralized counting center envisioned in the original package.[35] ECOWAS then endorsed and enacted the revised Special Law, including a new timetable for implementation and a new (reduced) budget.[36] The July 19 date left only two months for preparations—a very tight schedule given the state of planning and the logistical challenges facing the commission. A very basic system with simple registration and voting procedures was designed to make the timetable possible. Little time was available for voters' education or to conduct training of election officials.

The Campaign and Voter Registration

The thirty-day campaign period began on June 16, and a number of candidates held rallies in different parts of the country. Sirleaf and Taylor both opened their campaigns in Nimba County, reflecting a direct competition for key constituencies. Sirleaf's rally in Ganta was disrupted by violence that left several injured. Two former commanders in Taylor's NPFL were held by ECOMOG as a result of this incident. ECOMOG commander Malu met with the political parties on June 24 and threatened to respond with force against anyone initiating political violence: "While ECOMOG is escorting anyone to campaign, if you throw stones at that person, you will be throwing stones at ECOMOG and, as such, ECOMOG will retaliate by throwing bullets (at you)."[37] In the end, intimidation did not prevent the major candidates from campaigning in the countryside to the extent that time, money, and logistics permitted. In the vote-rich area around Monrovia (and to a degree in Buchanan, the second largest city), all candidates had the opportunity to campaign and a range of FM radio stations and newspapers representing diverse political views were available.

As the campaign unfolded, it became apparent to most observers that Sirleaf posed the strongest challenge to Taylor with the remaining parties having the potential to force a runoff if no candidate won more than 50 percent in the first round. Both candidates spoke of reconciliation, reconstruction, and economic revival, but the campaign did not stress differences in platforms. As one Western reporter characterized the choice for Liberia's voters, "Should they support a warrior who has the power to make the result stick? Or should they opt for a civilian, and run the risk that the defeated warlords will go back to the bush and restart the war?"[38] Many Liberians were convinced that Taylor would return to war if he lost the election, ECOMOG not withstanding. Sirleaf's campaign pointed out the atrocities associated with Taylor during the war, including producing posters with photographs of corpses and the caption "Chucky Did It." Without the ability to persuade voters that she could contain such violence if she won, these campaign images may have frightened more voters into casting their ballots for Taylor.

Taylor campaigned extensively throughout the country, using his resources to lease a helicopter to reach areas in the Southeast cut off by the rainy season. Sirleaf's campaign had more modest funds but held a number of rallies in the populous region around Monrovia and in Grand Bassa, Margibi, Bong, and Nimba counties.[39] Taylor and Sirleaf also held large but peaceful rallies near each other in Monrovia on July 17, the final day of campaigning.

The IECOM struggled through a number of crises in June, relating to the hiring of election officials, the deployment of county magistrates, and a rapid training period for registration and polling officials. The onset of the rainy season made large areas of the Southeast inaccessible by road, along with large parts of upper and lower Lofa County. Basic demographic data was guess work, few voters had documentation to prove their age or nationality, and many of the old registration and polling sites had been destroyed during the war. Despite numerous snags, the process kept moving along, building up momentum as time went on.

Registration began on June 24 in a disorganized manner.[40] The IECOM worked through problems caused by poor planning and agreed to extend the deadline for registration until July 3. Some Liberians alleged that underage people were registering and that registration cards were available for sale, but no one presented credible evidence of large-scale, organized fraud. ECOMOG provided security at each registration site and generally was regarded by the political parties and election officials as neutral. Despite hurried training, registration workers seemed to understand the process and demonstrated enormous dedication despite the harsh conditions and delayed payment of their salaries. According to IECOM, 751,430 people registered to vote. Fewer voters registered in Monrovia and the Montserrado County area than expected, and a late upsurge in registration in Taylor's strongholds in Bong and Nimba counties raised some concerns about the registration list. Insufficient registration materials in parts of upper Lofa County prevented some residents from registering. Despite these problems, the overwhelming majority of Liberians in the country had a reasonable opportunity to register.

International observers, particularly UNOMIL, visited most registration sites. Although party agents had the right to observe registration, only NPP was sufficiently organized and financed to deploy nationwide. Complications and confusion over credentials for party agents further limited observation of the registration process. In any event, few prospective voters were challenged at registration, and those rejected were usually disqualified on the basis of being under age.

International Participation

The Liberian government lacked the resources to conduct the election and getting even token payments out of the factionally divided

Council of State was difficult. A diverse range of international donors supported the process and demonstrated the capacity of international assistance to support the conduct of elections under extremely adverse circumstances. The United States Agency for International Development (USAID) provided funding to the International Foundation for Election Systems (IFES), a U.S.-based nongovernmental organization with extensive experience, for technical assistance and for the purchase of election commodities (ballot papers, forms, ink, and so forth).[41] The IFES also managed subgrants from USAID to various nongovernmental organizations, including The Carter Center and the Friends of Liberia to conduct observation missions, Refugee Policy Group to make an assessment on participation of refugees, returnees, and displaced persons in the election, the Academy for Educational Development for workshops on women's participation, and Fondation Hirondelle to establish Star Radio, an independent shortwave station.[42] The National Democratic Institute received USAID funding for civic education and to assist the Liberian Elections Observers Network (LEON), a coalition of fifteen domestic organizations that fielded approximately 1,200 observers on election day.[43] The International Republican Institute conducted training workshops for political party poll watchers. The U.S.-based NGO Search for Common Ground managed a radio production program through its Talking Drum Studio that developed popular broadcasts on topics relating to the election and postconflict reconciliation. The European Union provided funding for civic education, payments to election workers, technical assistance, and logistical support as well as fielding an observation mission.

The United Nations played multiple and potentially contradictory roles during the Liberian transition. UNOMIL had a mixed mandate and was an experiment in chapter VIII peacekeeping whereby a regional organization, in this case ECOWAS, took the lead. The international community failed to provide UNOMIL with resources adequate for the complex tasks assigned in the difficult environment of postwar Liberia. UNOMIL made do with leftover vehicles from other UN missions and secondhand communications equipment.[44] The UN job was complicated further by a change in its leadership in mid-April as the ineffective Anthony Nyaki was replaced as special representative of the secretary general by the Namibian diplomat Tuliameni Kalomoh.

Following its mandate to verify the disarmament process, UNOMIL's next mandate was to observe the election. The United Nations placed thirty-four civilian medium-term electoral observers into the sixteen field stations initially established for its military observers. Civilian and military observers deployed as teams during the pre-election period and played an important role in collecting information on demographics, road conditions, and possible locations for registration and polling sites. As a chapter VIII operation, UNOMIL and ECOWAS were mandated to jointly certify the election. This task not only required some subtle coordination of institutional perspectives but also raised questions about the extent to which the role ECOMOG peacekeepers played during the election could be evaluated.

UNOMIL's secondary mandate included providing limited logistical support to IECOM. As the election date approached, however, UNOMIL diverted more and more of its already overstretched resources to support the electoral process and to assist the county magistrates to prepare for registration and voting. UNOMIL's transportation and communication network was the only means for many regional election workers to move around and to transmit and receive information. ECOMOG also provided some logistical and transportation assistance to IECOM. Some worried that UNOMIL and ECOMOG's significant involvement in facilitating the work of the commission would interfere with their ability to observe and certify the results.

ECOWAS insisted on playing the lead role in managing the election, arguing that it had earned that right by shouldering the difficult burden of peacekeeping over the previous seven years. ECOWAS and the Nigerians in particular seemed to fear that the West was trying to "steal" the credit for the election. Suspicions and tensions relating to Nigeria's contentious relations with the international community in general complicated cooperation with relation to Liberia. Nigerian Foreign Minister and ECOWAS envoy Chief Tom Ikimi stated that the July 19 elections were "ECOWAS elections" and that international donors should provide funding but not interfere. As a result, it often was difficult for international donors to provide assistance and technical advice to the elections commission. In May, for example, IECOM would not provide IFES or the European Union with the draft Special Elections Package, making assistance in designing training materials or registration forms impossible. The budget remained uncertain and contentious, with ECOWAS, IECOM, and the international donors often having different understandings of commitments.

The IECOM and international donors learned many lessons from the difficult registration period, and concerted efforts to improve coordination and logistical plans were made. In particular, a logistics working group that brought together IECOM, the United Nations, IFES, the European Union, and ECOMOG worked to manage the deployment of materials for election day. Despite tensions between the donors and ECOWAS, coordination at the working level among IECOM, ECOMOG, and the international community developed well.

THE JULY 19, 1997, ELECTIONS

In the days before the election, Taylor and Sirleaf acted and spoke as if they expected to win, and many observers predicted that neither would gain a majority on the first round, making a runoff necessary. Although some have questioned the involvement of nongovernmental organizations such as The Carter Center and the Friends of Liberia in observing the election while the playing field remained decidedly tilted, it is worth noting that Sirleaf and other Liberian politicians with a lot more at stake regarded the election as important. Analysts of Liberian politics had a wide range of assessments on the eve of voting. Some suggested that Taylor would win overwhelmingly and pointed to his massive rallies late in the campaign period and his organizational capacity. Others, however, recalled how Liberians had voted against the authoritarian Samuel Doe in 1985 despite his control over the media and security forces and suggested that an upset was possible. The fact that individuals accepted NPP-distributed rice and T-shirts did not mean that the recipients would vote for the party.[45] Still others expected Taylor to win a plurality but not a majority. Under that scenario, a runoff would be necessary, presumably with Sirleaf who might win the "anybody but Taylor" votes and win the election. In contrast to many elections, particularly in Africa, considerable uncertainty about the outcome continued in the days immediately preceding the vote.

On election day, July, 19, 1997, voters turned out in large numbers, with an estimated 85 percent of the registered voting.[46] Nearly every polling station opened approximately on time, and nearly all had sufficient voting materials.[47] Most voters cast their ballots early in the day with large numbers already in line when the polls opened. Most polling sites had multiple party poll watchers as well as local observers organized by LEON and the Liberian Council of Churches. International and local observers and party poll watchers reported an extremely orderly process with only minor problems that did not affect the results.

ECOMOG provided security in nearly every polling station. In Monrovia, ECOMOG commander Victor Malu promised "reassurance to those in need of reassurance and warning to those in need of warning."[48] In many cases, the lack of voters' education and the high illiteracy rate resulted in voters needing considerable guidance in the polling place, raising some questions of undue influence.[49] A number of international observers were uncomfortable with the direct involvement of ECOMOG soldiers in the administration of the polling place.[50] In general, however, most observers concluded that the assistance was designed to speed up the process, not to alter the outcome.

Approximately 500 international observers watched the election and generally commended the process. UNOMIL, which had 34 civilian electoral observers deployed at sixteen sites throughout the country conducting medium-term observation, added approximately 200 short-term observers on election day.[51] The Carter Center fielded 40 observers, led by President Jimmy Carter, President Nicéphore Soglo, the former president of Benin and former chair of ECOWAS, and former U.S. Senator Paul Simon. The Carter Center group concluded that "the election represents a very important step forward for Liberia."[52] The Friends of Liberia, a U.S.-based nongovernmental organization founded by former Peace Corps volunteers who had served in Liberia, fielded 34 observers and concluded that "despite problems, this process was free, fair, and transparent."[53] The European Union and the Organization of African Unity similarly concluded that the elections were free and fair. UNOMIL and ECOWAS issued a joint certification, as required by their chapter VIII mandate, that "declared that the electoral process . . . was free, fair, and credible."[54] LEON, the Liberian domestic observing group, made a positive preliminary statement as well.

Logistical difficulties prevented IECOM from announcing final results as quickly as called for in the Special Elections Law. After some hesitation and under pressure from the international community, IECOM decided to release preliminary results as they were available. Early returns from Montserrado County, the area around Monrovia where Sirleaf and the civilian candidates had been expected to do best, indicated that Taylor was in the lead even before votes in his base (Bong, Nimba counties) were counted.

Some Unity Party leaders protested that IECOM and ECOMOG engaged in fraud.[55] Alhaji Kromah's ALCOP and George Boley's NDPL also claimed that the results were not credible and charged massive irregularities.[56] None of the parties, however, presented specific evidence to validate their charges, and few made a distinction between irregularities attributable to poor training and an over-extended administration as distinct from electoral fraud that could have changed the final results. As the size of Taylor's margin became more apparent and positive observer reports were issued, Sirleaf moderated her statements and urged her supporters to prepare for a role as a "strong and constructive opposition."[57] Taylor decided not to make any victory pronouncement until the results were officially proclaimed and there were no large public demonstrations or celebrations.

According to official results, Taylor won the presidency with more than 75 percent of the vote, followed by Sirleaf with 9.6 percent. In the Senate, the National Patriotic Party won twenty-one seats, the Unity Party three seats, and the All Liberian Coalition Party two seats. In the House of Representatives, the NPP won forty-nine seats, UP won seven, ALCOP three, the Alliance of Political Parties two, the United People's Party two, and the Liberian People's Party one (see table A-1).[58]

On August 2, 1997, Taylor was sworn in as president of Liberia. Eight West African heads of state attended the ceremony, including Sani Abacha of Nigeria and Henri Konan Bedie of Côte d'Ivoire.[59] Taylor promised in his inaugural address to establish a human rights and reconciliation commission and emphasized his intention to govern as the president of all Liberians. NPP members dominated Taylor's cabinet, but he also included several former rivals (such as Roosevelt Johnson, Tom Woewiyu, and Francois Massaquoi) in relatively minor posts, such as Rural Development, Labour, and Youth and Sports.

UNDERSTANDING THE RESULTS

Numerous factors contributed to the NPP's overwhelming victory in the 1997 Liberian election.[60] Taylor successfully converted his NPFL military faction into the NPP, an effective political machine. Nearly every town in Liberia and every constituency in Monrovia had an NPP office, and the country was covered in Taylor signs, bumper stickers, and T-shirts. Taylor's NPFL had operated as the de facto government in much of Liberia for years, and his organization therefore had a network throughout the countryside that was unmatched by his rivals.

Taylor also had far greater resources than his competitors. In a country with few vehicles, Taylor brought in Land Rovers, buses, motorcycles, loudspeaker trucks, and leased a helicopter. Taylor controlled the formerly state-owned shortwave radio station and thereby dominated the airwaves through which most Liberians outside of Monrovia received their news. The NPP distributed rice to prospective voters and used patronage extensively to demonstrate its capacity to provide needed resources. While the code of conduct adopted as part of the Special Elections Package placed limits on campaign spending, the lack of enforcement mechanisms allowed Taylor to spend freely. No attempts were made to force Taylor to give up resources seized during the war, such as the state-owned radio, before the campaign.

Taylor campaigned widely and his rallies matched political speeches with popular entertainments, including music, dance, fashion shows, and games. After so many years of grim warfare, Taylor's campaign offered excitement and a return to the normal pleasures of the past. Taylor was a master of highly public generosity and won publicity by paying to fly Liberia's national soccer team to the African Nations Cup tournament, funding the Charles Ghankay Taylor Educational and Humanitarian Relief Foundation, and donating ambulances to the John F. Kennedy Hospital in Monrovia.[61] In his speeches, Taylor promised new programs to address the full range of social needs. His populist message resonated with many of Liberia's poor who regarded Sirleaf as the candidate of the educated elite. In some parts of Liberia, Taylor was a popular figure who was remembered for defending their communities against attacks from rival militias and who maintained relative order in his zone of military occupation during the war.

While financial and organizational advantages were critically important, they also were well known to competing political parties and to international donors months before the election. Furthermore, these advantages were least important in populous Montserrado County, where easy transportation, FM radio, and a wide variety of newspapers were available. Taylor won Montserrado County with 55 percent of the vote to Sirleaf's 22 percent, suggesting that far more than the resource imbalance explained the landslide.

Perhaps most important, memories of seven years of brutal conflict and the consequent fear shaped how voters viewed the election and the choices available to them. As one observer put it, the voters "were intimidated not by thugs at the polling stations but by the trauma of the last seven years of war."[62] The issue of peace dominated the July 1997 election, and most voters seemed determined to use their franchise to maximize the chances of stability. Many Liberians believed that if Taylor lost the election the country would return to war.[63] Taylor's rivals pointed out his violent past during the campaign but could not propose credible actions to contain him if he challenged the results. With ineffective demobilization, weak measures to prevent a spoiler from challenging the results, and statements from ECOWAS reiterating its intention to leave Liberia quickly after the voting, voters risked conflict if Taylor did not win the election.[64]

In addition, many Liberians wanted a strong leader capable of maintaining order and containing the forces of rival factions. Seven years of weak interim governments convinced many Liberians that only a unified government could keep the peace, and Taylor was perceived as the candidate most likely to bring strong government. Many voters said they did not care who won so long as a single president ruled the country again and the period of interim government ended. Despite his participation in the Council of State, Taylor effectively ran as a challenger against the incumbent government and blamed it for Liberia's economic and social problems.

In contrast to Taylor's well-organized campaign, the civilian opposition candidates ran very poor races. Squabbling among civilian candidates, some of whom were associated with failed governments of the past, did not elicit confidence from voters looking for strong leadership. The acrimonious collapse of the Alliance of Political Parties discredited several political figures and their associated parties.[65] Sheikh Konneh, a leader of Liberia's religious community, stated after the election that "those who claimed to be civilian politicians apparently failed to carry out their homework well. Hence, they should have no one to blame for their own dereliction."[66] The Unity Party had difficulty convincing worried voters that if Sirleaf won she could contain renewed attacks from Taylor or other defeated factions. In an election dominated by the voters' search for security, the perception that Sirleaf could not withstand an attack from a losing faction made it very difficult for her to win substantial support.

Two issues relating to the electoral system in Liberia also played a part in the size of Taylor's margin. The quick timetable may have favored the candidate with the best organization. The opposition had insufficient time to get its message out and inform the voters of their choice.[67] Finally, the decision endorsed by all political parties in the May summit in Abuja to have a single ballot may have favored Taylor by denying voters the chance to vote for Taylor for president on one ballot and balance that vote by selecting an alternative slate from a different party for the legislature.

Few if any who watched in horror the brutality and violence that exploded in Monrovia in April 1996 predicted or even dreamed that a peaceful and relatively well-run election resulting in a return to constitutional rule would be possible just sixteen months later. Given the extraordinarily difficult challenges Liberia presented, the fact that voters across the country had an opportunity to play a role in bringing about a transition without further violence was a remarkable accomplishment. These same challenges, and the legacy of destruction and distrust that arose from seven years of vicious combat, however, suggested that far more than a single successful election would be necessary to bring about the dual goals of genuine conflict resolution and sustainable democratization.

4

LESSONS FROM
THE LIBERIAN ELECTIONS

The July 19, 1997, elections in Liberia represented an impressive demonstration of the Liberian people's desire for peace. Large numbers turned out to register, stood patiently in long lines in order to vote, and waited calmly for official results to be announced. Relatively minor problems during the campaign period, registration process, and on election day did not alter the overall results.

For elections to be fully meaningful, however, they must give voters a significant choice. In the 1997 Special Elections in Liberia, many voters understood their choice as being between Charles Taylor, the former factional leader, and war, clearly an unenviable range of options. Given the legacy of the recent conflict and the pervasive fear that Taylor would return to war if not elected, many Liberians made a calculated choice that they hoped would more likely promote peace and stability. One Liberian summed up a general attitude when he said, "He [Taylor] killed my father but I'll vote for him. He started all this and he's going to fix it."[1] While a significant number of voters identified with Taylor and his populist message or patronage, many seemed cautious, war-weary, and determined to use their vote to appease the powerful ex-factional leader.

REFLECTIONS ON THE ELECTIONS

The July 19, 1997, Special Elections ratified and institutionalized the political topography and imbalance of power created by seven years of war. Taylor's National Patriotic Front of Liberia (NPFL) dominated much of the country from 1990; after the election his National Patriotic Party (NPP) controlled the government. The process by which Taylor's power gained legitimacy, however, mattered. Taylor won greater international, regional, and local acceptance for his government through a process of elections, not through a unilateral military victory or a negotiated agreement among factional elites and regional powers. In order to win the election, Taylor converted his military organization into an effective mass mobilizing political party, replacing guns with patronage and roadblocks with rallies. The speed of this conversion and the ineffective demobilization process, however, leaves in place doubts about the democratic character of Taylor's organizational base.

The electoral process furthermore allowed Liberians to play their roles as voters, not as powerless victims facing a mighty armed force. As a result, the Liberian people won a greater standing to assert their rights as citizens responsible for legitimizing Taylor's power.[2] The new political order provided an opportunity for rival groups to play their roles as opposition parties within a legal framework rather than as defeated factions without rights. In addition, the election and return to constitutional rule placed legal limits around the new regime's power. The extent to which the new administration will adhere to constitutional constraints and pay attention to the voters who brought them to power, however, remains open. Furthermore, the Liberian constitution concentrates power in the office of the presidency and gives the new government a six-year term in office before it must face the voters again.

In addition, the electoral period provided the international community with an opportunity to fund programs that may support democratization in the long term. The funding by the U.S. Agency for International Development (USAID) for domestic election observers helped strengthen these organizations and may allow them to play a more forceful role in demanding accountability from the new government. The agency also provided financial support to Star Radio, an independent radio station. Star Radio did not get on the air until the last moment before the elections, preventing it from playing an important role in balancing the uneven access among political parties to the media. The radio's continued operation, however, can reinforce accountability and assist in the development of freedom of the press.

As with constitutional constraints, however, the ability of civil society and independent media to resist pressures from a determined and powerful government are limited.

While an election following a period of conflict may be insufficient to reverse military power on the ground, the process of voting may allow the people to express their insistence that power can only be made legitimate through popular participation. Ancillary benefits that support long-term democratization, ranging from party building, the development of domestic nongovernmental organizations, and greater freedom of the media, developed as a result of the election. Taylor could not be defeated, but he also could not rule with legitimate authority until voting took place and the Liberian people had an opportunity to have a voice.

It is also possible that the July 1997 election, rather than providing the basis for future democratization, may serve to strengthen the authoritarian leaders who institutionalized their power by winning the vote. Taylor and the NPP may use their new positions to entrench their power, limit political freedom, and make it less likely that future elections will be competitive. Furthermore, the precedent of an election that took place under conditions of a distinctly unlevel playing field and in which voters perceived very limited choice may delegitimize future elections in the eyes of many Liberians. Cynicism about democracy and the role of elections that derive from a flawed process may make it more difficult to convince voters that subsequent contests may be more meaningful.

The July 1997 election may have played an important role in implementing the Abuja peace process, but its part in a broader process of building a sustainable peace is less certain. An election held in the context of an imperfect peace agreement should not be held responsible for the imperfections of that framework. The Abuja Accord represented a minimal agreement to end the fighting, bring in a constitutional government, and allow regional peacekeepers to withdraw with little attention to the longer and more difficult problems of reconciliation and the rebuilding of social relationships necessary to promote long-term conflict management.[3] An agreement to end the fighting without addressing the deeper issues of reconciliation may result in a brief interregnum before a new round of conflict.

In many ways, the Liberian election resembled a referendum on peace, with Taylor perceived as the candidate most capable of preventing a return to war. The domination of the future government by a single party, however, will raise concerns among many Liberians that the war ended not in an inclusive government of reconciliation but with an exclusive victory for one of the warring parties. Furthermore, for sustainable democracy to take root, future elections will need to be held in a context in which voters have sufficient security and information to have a broader range of choice.

POSTELECTION PROSPECTS

Postconflict elections, as suggested in chapter 1, have twin goals relating to war termination and democratization. The July 1997 Special Elections in Liberia represented a step forward with relation to war termination but had only a marginal role in encouraging democratization. Even as a mechanism of war termination, however, it remains to be seen how sustainable the new institutions legitimized by the election will be in preventing a resurgence of violence. With the inauguration of the new regime, at least the potential for stability emerged. The old Council of State had demonstrated its inability to manage the difficult challenges facing Liberia. The eventual behavior of the new leaders remained undetermined and thereby subject to incentives from the international community. Although the ultimate outcome of the NPP administration remains to be seen, warnings from comparative postconflict cases and from Taylor's past behavior suggest that constitutional constraints on power and the ability of voters to hold their leaders accountable often are not sufficient. In its first few months in office, the new regime's record was mixed, with a number of developments providing continuing grounds for concern.

Taylor's government faced tremendous hurdles following its inauguration. The treasury reportedly contained $17,000 while the government had $200 million in domestic debt (notably back wages for civil servants who had not been paid in many cases for over a year) and $2 billion in external debt.[4] The country continued to use two separate currencies, an artifact of the wartime division, and financial institutions were either nonexistent or under the control of special interests. Refugees were beginning to return, but little was in place in the countryside in terms of housing or jobs to receive them. As one journalist summarized the situation, "There is no public power supply, less than a tenth of the entire national road network is accessible by vehicles, education and health services are in ruins and a demoralized civil service, which has not been paid salaries for months, runs the government."[5] Instability from neighboring Sierra Leone where ECOMOG intervened following a 1997 coup threatened to spill over the border once again. Conditions in Liberia would challenge any government.

While the regime established a human rights commission and appointed Taylor's former factional rival Alhaji Kromah to a reconciliation commission, other incidents raised fears. Harassment of the media suggested that the new regime will resist accountability and not allow criticism.[6] International observers applauded some government appointments, such as the selection of former World Bank official Elias Saleeby as minister of finance and Gloria Scott as chief justice of the Supreme Court, but observers expressed concerns about other appointments, such as old NPFL stalwarts Joe Tate as chief of police and Joe Mulbah as information minister. The December 1997 murder of Sam Dokie (one of Taylor's early supporters who then broke with the NPFL and joined the Unity Party in 1997), while he was in the custody of Taylor's security forces, led many Liberians to fear that the violence of the war years was not over yet.[7] Kromah, the chair of the reconciliation commission, went abroad and, citing fear for his life, refused to return to Liberia. He was replaced by Victoria Reffell, an old ally of Taylor. Tensions flared between Taylor and Roosevelt Johnson, the Krahn leader who left his cabinet post, went abroad for a period, and then returned to Monrovia. The economic challenges of reconstruction remained daunting, and the international donors and international financial institutions appeared skeptical and hesitant.[8]

The role of ECOMOG within Liberia following the elections added to the difficulties. Although the Abuja II Accord mandated ECOMOG to build a restructured Armed Forces of Liberia, Taylor asserted his rights as duly elected head of state to create his own military. Victor Malu, ECOMOG chief, stated that ECOWAS had a responsibility to reform the army because the winner of the election could be accused of transforming his faction into an army and that "this is happening now."[9] Taylor and Malu failed to reach a mutually acceptable modus vivendi and Malu was replaced in January 1998 by Maj. Gen. Timothy Shelpidi from Nigeria. Taylor undertook to reform the armed forces on his own. Many reported that the new security forces were filled with old NPFL fighters, while other groups, particularly the

Krahn, were systematically purged from the army.[10] In May 1998, 2,000 dismissed members of the Armed Forces of Liberia staged violent demonstrations until contained by ECOMOG soldiers.[11]

The U.S. government reacted cautiously to the unexpected Taylor victory. Few seemingly anticipated his landslide, and some had difficulty in reconciling a "free" election and the victory of a leader implicated in the atrocities of the war. The administration accepted that Taylor was the new leader and offered assistance tied to a series of benchmarks, particularly human rights and the creation of an independent judiciary and professional police force. Official donors and international nongovernmental organizations, however, responded cautiously and slowly. James Bishop, former U.S. ambassador to Liberia, stated that "given [Taylor's] track record, one would be foolish to proclaim himself an optimist."[12]

Regardless of the longer-term outcome, the implementation of the Abuja Accord through the July 1997 elections transformed the nature of politics in Liberia. If the elections usher in an era of stability, the Abuja peace process will have succeeded in putting in place a formula to end the Liberian civil war. An assessment on whether it served as the beginning of a democratic era will have to wait until future elections in which the voters are given a choice among viable candidates rather than a choice between war and peace.

SUPPORTING POSTCONFLICT ELECTIONS

The Liberian case demonstrates the multiple uses of elections in the current international environment. Although elections are inherently and logically connected to ideas of peaceful competition, participation, accountability, and other attributes of democracy, they may also perform other important roles. In Liberia, the ability of elections to serve as a mechanism to initiate a process of democratization was limited, but their ability to terminate a particular period of conflict and to serve as a diplomatic stratagem to permit ECOWAS and Nigeria to disengage from their position opposing Charles Taylor was important.

The 1993 elections in Cambodia similarly served a number of purposes, including furthering the marginalization of the Khmer Rouge and providing a mechanism for external powers to cut their ties to clients in the region. The election's role in advancing democracy was less clear, given the manner by which Hun Sen and the Cambodian Peoples Party retained power despite losing the election and their 1997 coup d'etat against Prince Norodom Ranariddh and the royalist coalition that won the 1993 election. The Bosnian elections of September 1996 were important with regard to the international implementation force (IFOR) put in place to enforce the Dayton Agreement. Furthermore, the conclusion of this phase of the Dayton peace process created an internationally recognized regime, a critical requirement for international financial institutions and donors who require partners to initiate their lending. The relationship between the elections and the promotion of democracy, however, remained far less certain.[13]

These partial successes are often criticized and characterized as failures because the process of democratization did not advance significantly or may have suffered a setback. This criticism is largely accurate but misses an important dimension of postconflict transitions. As recent studies have suggested, many factors are necessary for a postconflict election to advance the processes of war termination and democratization. The nature of the conflict, the character of transitional institutions and parties to the conflict, the availability of time, resources, and security to rebuild peacetime social structures, and the effectiveness of international support all shape the chances for success, as outlined in chapter 1.

In Liberia and in many other cases, however, these elements were not present. This is unfortunate, and the international community should examine what it might have done in order to create a more propitious context for a given peace process. Regardless of the cause, however, when policymakers are faced with making recommendations in a case that lacks the components most likely to promote sustainable war termination and democratization, they must accept that the best they can do is to select the "least bad" options then available. The Liberian case suggests that for the international community to accept and provide the financial resources necessary to make possible a flawed election that stops the fighting and moves the political process into a new phase is worth doing. Policymakers charged with addressing the massive challenges that face postconflict societies cannot afford to make successful democratization the criteria for all policies and must accept that in many of these hard cases war termination may be the only available short-term option that at least provides the potential for long-term stability and eventual transition to more liberal and democratic governance. To set expectations too high may lead policymakers to miss opportunities to assist in managing conflict.

The timing of postconflict elections is critical to the capacity of such events to promote the dual goals of war termination and democratization. In some cases, the pace of implementation may be different for the two distinct challenges. Democratization requires time and will be encouraged by a slower timetable that places elections at the end of a sequence of events such as demilitarization, repatriation of refugees and displaced, and rebuilding the basics of a functioning state. War termination, however, may require a more rapid pace to obtain the consent of the warring parties and to build momentum from a cease-fire. Waiting too long may lead to the collapse of the peace process and a return to war. Policies relating to demilitarization, repatriation, and reconstruction—and indeed, democratization—may need to wait until after the peace agreement has been implemented and the fighting ended. Whether the international community should press for a longer transition and a realistic opportunity to accomplish the dual goals of war termination and democratization simultaneously or accept that the former must be quick will be case specific and will require difficult judgments about the nature of the peace agreement. If war termination cannot wait, then the international community should accept this limited but vitally important goal since ending the fighting is a prerequisite for democratization and the other attributes of postconflict reconstruction and reconciliation.

Even in cases where war termination requires a rapid pace, ending the brief transition in an election rather than some other mechanism to ratify the new regime may deliver ancillary benefits that can promote long-term democratization. Elections provide openings for the international community to support programs that encourage a variety of developments that support peaceful political competition. As was seen in the Liberian case, the elections encouraged the transformation of the militias into mass political parties. This important change also took place in Mozambique and El Salvador. In addition, the election marked a return to constitutional rule with at least legal limits on the new regime's power. This was also the case in Bosnia. Postconflict elections in Liberia and elsewhere allowed citizens to participate as voters and thereby gave them a larger role in their government than alternative mechanisms.

International donors used the opportunity of the elections in Liberia to fund programs to encourage civil society through projects in support of domestic observer groups. In Cambodia as well, the transition and election served as the context for a rapid development of domestic nongovernmental organizations. The United States used the election to launch an independent radio station in Liberia, a significant accomplishment with large implications for accountability and the development of a free press, given the partisan control of the major sources of news. The United Nations similarly sponsored an independent radio station in Cambodia during the transition. The sustainability of these projects and the ability of independent media or civil society to resist antidemocratic moves, however, often is limited, as the 1997 coup in Cambodia demonstrated.

In other cases, postconflict elections have provided the opening for assistance to electoral infrastructure (the creation of voting lists, the training of election officials) and for civic education. This was true, to an extent at least, in Ethiopia where postconflict elections were not competitive, but reasonably effective electoral institutions were created. In Liberia, the rapid pace of the transition and limited resources prevented important gains in these areas.

The potential to achieve these limited but important potential benefits for long-term democratization by supporting flawed elections should be balanced against the potential for such elections to diminish the chances for sustaining a political opening by strengthening authoritarian leaders. If nondemocratic leaders win postconflict elections, as in Bosnia, Liberia, and elsewhere, they will have the opportunity to entrench their power and use state institutions to weaken their opponents and strengthen their hold on power. The ability of future elections to be competitive may be reduced if a de facto single-party government is created and legitimized by the first round of elections. In addition, if the public concludes that flawed elections indicate that voting is a tool by which powerful forces in society legitimize their control without offering the voter a meaningful choice and that the international community is prepared to sanctify such exercises as "free and fair," then distrust of democratic institutions will become pervasive. Flawed elections may be the "least bad" alternative in a postconflict environment, but the price for long-term democratization may be high.

For the international community to recognize the opportunity to support war termination elections in contexts where democratization will receive at best a modest boost, policymakers and analysts will have to accept that elections can serve multiple purposes. The traditional judgment on elections—were they "free and fair?"—should give way to a more nuanced and contextual interpretation.[14] Free and fair elections are important, but under the difficult circumstances of postconflict transitions a more immediate judgment may be whether the elections were meaningful or effective with relation to war termination goals. The tendency to define an election as a success or failure on the basis of democracy alone risks distorting the meaning of democracy by characterizing elections that have little to do with choice as "democratic."[15] In cases like Angola, elections characterized as "free and fair" by international observers failed miserably with respect to war termination. In other cases, notably El Salvador and Mozambique, the election succeeded to advance both goals of war termination and democratization. In Liberia, the election should be understood as marking an important stage in transforming the conflict (with the long-term sustainability of conflict management still in doubt) while failing to advance significantly the democratization process.

APPENDIX

AFL   Armed Forces of Liberia

ECOMOG   ECOWAS Cease-Fire Monitoring Group

ECOWAS   Economic Community of West African States, consisting of Benin, Burkina Faso, Cape Verde, Côte d'Ivoire, Gambia, Ghana, Guinea, Guinea-Bissau, Liberia, Mali, Mauritania, Niger, Nigeria, Senegal, Sierra Leone, and Togo

IECOM   Independent Elections Commission

IGNU   Interim Government of National Unity

LNTG   Liberian National Transitional Government

LPC   Liberia Peace Council

LPP   Liberian People's Party

NDPL   National Democratic Party of Liberia

NPFL   National Patriotic Front of Liberia

NPFL-CDC   National Patriotic Front of Liberia—Central Revolutionary Council

NPP   National Patriotic Party

NPRAG   National Patriotic Reconstruction Assembly
Government

OAU   Organization of African Unity

RUF   Revolutionary United Front

ULIMO   United Liberation Movement of Liberia for
Democracy

ULIMO-J   United Liberation Movement of Liberia for
Democracy—Johnson

ULIMO-K   United Liberation Movement of Liberia for
Democracy—Kromah

UNOMIL   United Nations Observer Mission in Liberia

THE MAIN LIBERIAN AND INTERNATIONAL ACTORS

ALLIANCE OF POLITICAL PARTIES   The Alliance of Political
Parties was formed in 1996 with the hope of providing a united
slate to compete against the factional leaders. Following a contentious convention the alliance selected Cletus Wortoson as its
standard bearer. It won 2.6 percent of the vote and two seats in the
House of Representatives.

ALL LIBERIAN COALITION PARTY (ALCOP)   The party created
by Alhaji Kromah following the disbanding of his ULIMO-K faction. Kromah and his party won 4 percent of the vote in July 1997,
with its strongest showing in Lofa County. The ALCOP secured two
seats in the Senate and three in the House of Representatives.

ARMED FORCES OF LIBERIA (AFL)   The armed forces of Samuel
Doe, largely recruited from the Krahn ethnic group, remained loyal
to Doe until his death in 1990. Thereafter elements of the AFL
fought with ULIMO and LPC. The AFL was confined to its barracks
under the Bamako cease-fire but was reactivated to help repulse
Taylor from Monrovia in late 1992.

**THE ECONOMIC COMMUNITY OF WEST AFRICAN STATES
CEASE-FIRE MONITORING GROUP (ECOMOG)**   This regional
military force intervened in Liberia in August 1990 to observe a
cease-fire but quickly became drawn into peace enforcement and

major confrontation with the NPFL. The bulk of the finance and personnel came from Nigeria, but Ghana, Senegal, Burkina Faso, Sierra Leone, Guinea, and Benin also contributed troops at various times. Often collaborating with the AFL, LPC, and ULIMO, the multilateral forces in ECOMOG struggled to contain the NPFL and general disorder. In 1997 new leadership, and increased assistance from the United States and Europe, created a more effective military force.

INDEPENDENT NATIONAL PATRIOTIC FRONT OF LIBERIA (INPFL) A breakaway NPFL faction led by Prince Yormie Johnson, this front controlled parts of Monrovia in 1990 but faded in 1991 and was formally disbanded in 1992.

INTERIM GOVERNMENT OF NATIONAL UNITY (IGNU) Created by ECOWAS in August 1990 and protected by ECOMOG, IGNU served as the governing authority in Monrovia until it was replaced by the Liberian National Transitional Government in 1993. This government was led by Amos Sawyer and included a number of prominent civilian politicians from the Liberian People's Party.

LIBERIAN NATIONAL TRANSITIONAL GOVERNMENT (LNTG) Established by the Cotonou Accord in 1993, this government was formed by a five-member council and cabinet appointed by the factional leaders.

LIBERIA PEACE COUNCIL (LPC) The LPC emerged in 1993, following the Cotonou Accord, and fought the NPFL in southeastern Liberia. A predominantly Krahn organization led by George Boley.

LIBERIAN PEOPLE'S PARTY (LPP) Led by long-time political and community activist Togba-Nah Tipoteh, the LPP won 1.6 percent of the votes in the July 1997 elections and secured one seat in the House of Representatives.

LOFA DEFENSE FORCE (LDF) Led by Francois Massaquoi, this group resisted ULIMO-K control in parts of Lofa County in early 1994.

NATIONAL PATRIOTIC FRONT OF LIBERIA (NPFL) Led by Charles Taylor, the NPFL launched the war in December 1989. During most of the war it occupied most of Liberia and operated an alternative national administration, known as the National Patriotic Reconstruction Assembly Government (NPRAG) based in Gbarnga. The NPFL was officially disbanded in February 1997.

NATIONAL PATRIOTIC FRONT OF LIBERIA-CENTRAL REVOLUTIONARY COUNCIL (NPFL-CRC) A breakaway NPFL faction that emerged in 1994. Led by prominent NPFL figures Samuel Dokie and Tom Woewiyu, the NPFL-CRC fought with NPFL around Gbarnga.

NATIONAL PATRIOTIC PARTY (NPP) The party created by Charles Taylor after the NPFL disbanded. The NPP won over 75 percent of the vote in the July 1997 election and became the ruling party in Liberia.

UNITED LIBERATION MOVEMENT OF LIBERIA FOR DEMOCRACY (ULIMO) The ULIMO was founded by former AFL fighters in Sierra Leone and fought NPFL in western Liberia starting in September 1991. ULIMO broke into two wings in 1994, ULIMO-J, a Krahn faction led by Roosevelt Johnson and ULIMO-K, a Moslem/Mandingo faction led by Alhaji Kromah. Johnson did not participate in the 1997 elections while Kromah competed for the presidency as the standard-bearer of the All Liberia Coalition Party (ALCOP).

UNITED NATIONS OBSERVER MISSION IN LIBERIA (UNOMIL) Established in September 1993, following the Cotonou Accord, this mission was designed to respond to Charles Taylor's charges that ECOMOG was not neutral. It had a small military observer force and an electoral division that provided assistance and observed the 1997 elections.

UNITED PEOPLE'S PARTY (UPP) The UPP nominated Baccus Matthews as its candidate and won 2.5 percent of the vote in 1997, resulting in two seats in the House of Representatives.

UNITY PARTY This party selected Ellen Johnson Sirleaf as its presidential nominee in 1997. The Unity Party polled 9.6 percent of the vote, resulting in three seats in the Senate and seven in the House of Representatives. Sirleaf and the Unity Party received its largest share of votes from Montserrado County around Monrovia.

THE PEACE AGREEMENTS

THE BAMAKO CEASE-FIRE AGREEMENT November 28, 1990. The NPFL, AFL, and INPFL, the three active factions at the time, signed the agreement and committed themselves to a cease-fire, to participate in a national conference to establish a civilian-dominated interim government, and to elections to be held within twelve months.

LOMÉ AGREEMENT February 13, 1991. An elaboration of the Bamako Agreement that gave ECOMOG the lead role in disarming the factions.

YAMOUSSOUKRO I ACCORD June 30, 1991.

YAMOUSSOUKRO II ACCORD July 29, 1991.

YAMOUSSOUKRO III ACCORD September 17, 1991.

YAMOUSSOUKRO IV ACCORD October 30, 1991.

Under the leadership of President Houphouët Boigny of Côte d'Ivoire, the Yamoussoukro Agreements represented efforts to bridge the gaps between IGNU in Monrovia and Taylor's NPFL. Yamoussoukro IV included a cease-fire, a call for encampment of forces, and elections to be held within six months.

COTONOU ACCORD July 25, 1993. The most comprehensive accord of the Liberian peace process. It included provisions on cease-fire, the creation of a Liberian National Transitional Government to replace IGNU, and elections within six months. The ULIMO, a faction that had not signed earlier agreements, participated in the Cotonou talks.

AKOSOMBO AGREEMENT September 12, 1994. A supplement to the Cotonou Accord, the Akosombo Agreement expanded the role of the armed factions in managing Liberian state affairs.

ACCRA CLARIFICATION December 21, 1994. An expanded agreement that brought in a number of factions who did not participate in earlier agreements, namely, the Lofa Defence Force, the Liberian Peace Council, The NPFL-Central Revolutionary Council, the two wings of ULIMO (ULIMO-J and ULIMO-K), and a civilian representative of the Liberian National Conference.

ABUJA I ACCORD August 19, 1995. This agreement extended the Council of State by adding a civilian sixth member as chairman and redividing the various government posts among the factions.

ABUJA II ACCORD August 17, 1996. While the institutions remained the same, Abuja II included a new timetable and threatened sanctions against factional leaders who refused to implement their commitments.

TABLE A-1. Results of Liberia's National Elections, by County, July 1997

Percent voting for political party

County	PPP	NRP	FDP	LINU	UP	ALCOP	NPP	Alliance	RAP	PDPL	UPP	NDPL	LPP
Bomi	0.8	0.3	0.4	0.5	4.0	4.7	86.4	0.9	0.4	0.2	0.4	0.4	0.6
Bong	0.2	0.1	0.1	0.1	1.0	1.9	95.7	0.4	0.2	0.0	0.1	0.1	0.2
Grand Bassa	0.4	0.1	0.2	0.1	2.1	1.0	92.2	0.7	0.3	0.1	2.3	0.1	0.4
Cape Mount	0.8	7.4	0.7	0.4	7.5	3.6	74.0	2.8	0.7	0.2	0.5	0.7	0.8
Grand Gedeh	0.7	0.3	0.3	0.1	1.7	1.0	55.0	3.4	0.3	0.5	0.7	35.1	0.8
Grand Kru	0.7	0.3	0.4	0.5	2.5	0.7	72.3	2.0	0.7	9.0	1.2	0.2	9.6
Lofa	0.6	0.4	0.4	5.5	2.7	17.2	69.3	1.8	0.7	0.2	0.4	0.2	0.5
Margibi	0.1	0.2	0.2	0.4	4.0	1.2	92.0	0.5	0.2	0.1	0.9	0.1	0.1
Maryland	0.5	0.2	0.3	0.2	2.0	1.3	94.1	0.5	0.3	0.1	0.1	0.1	0.4
Montserrado	0.4	0.5	0.5	1.4	21.9	4.5	55.2	4.7	0.3	1.0	5.1	1.5	3.0
Nimba	0.0	0.0	0.0	0.0	0.4	1.9	96.5	0.8	0.1	0.0	0.1	0.0	0.1
Rivercess	0.6	0.2	0.4	0.4	4.9	0.9	78.3	1.2	0.9	0.3	10.8	0.2	0.7
Sinoe	0.4	0.3	0.7	0.3	14.4	1.1	50.1	8.0	0.7	0.4	8.9	3.8	10.8
Total	0.3	0.5	0.3	1.1	9.6	4.0	75.3	2.6	0.3	0.6	2.5	1.3	1.6

PPP, Progressive People's Party (Cheapoo, standard bearer), NRP, National Reformation Party (Sheriff), FDP, Free Democratic Party (Gbollie), LINU, Liberian National Union (Moniba), UP, Unity Party (Johnson-Sirleaf), ALCOP, All Liberian Coalition Party (Kromah), NPP, National Patriotic Party (Taylor), Alliance, Alliance of Political Parties (Wortoson), RAP, Reformation Alliance Party (Fahnbulleh), PDPL, People's Democratic Party of Liberia (Washington), UPP, United People's Party (Matthews), NDPL, National Democratic Party of Liberia (Boley), LPP, Liberian People's Party (Tipoteh).

Notes

Chapter 1

1. Krishna Kumar and Marina Ottaway, *From Bullets to Ballots: Electoral Assistance to Postconflict Societies* (Agency for International Development, Center for Development Information and Evaluation, 1997); and Krishna Kumar, ed., *Postconflict Elections, Democratization, and International Assistance* (Lynne Reiner, 1998). The findings of this study and the underlying case studies inform much of the analysis in this chapter.

2. Edward S. Herman and Frank Brodhead, *Demonstration Elections: U.S.-Staged Elections in the Dominican Republic, Vietnam, and El Salvador* (Boston: South End Press, 1984). See also Terry Karl, "Imposing Consent? Electoralism vs. Democratization in El Salvador," in Paul Drake and Eduardo Silva, eds., *Elections and Democratization in Latin America, 1980–85* (San Diego: CLAS/Center for US-Mexican Studies, 1986), pp. 9–36.

3. The antidemocratic moves by Second Prime Minister Hun Sen against First Prime Minister Prince Norodom Ranariddh in 1997 make the 1993 Cambodian election a difficult case to assess. A successful election is not a guarantee against subsequent backsliding but, to the extent that the 1997 crisis had its basis in the failure of the 1993 elections to result in sustainable institutions, the elections failed to promote democratization. See International Republican Institute and National Democratic Institute, "Restoring Democracy in Cambodia: The Difficult Road Ahead," Report of a Joint IRI-NDI Mission to Cambodia, August 29, 1997; and International Republican Institute and National Democratic Institute, "Political Conditions in Cambodia: Prospects for Free and Fair Elections," Report of the Second Joint NDI/IRI Assessment Mission, January 29, 1998.

4. On defining civil war see Roy Licklider, ed., *Stopping the Killing: How Civil Wars End* (New York University Press, 1993), pp. 9–10. Many analysts, however, would count South Africa as a civil war.

5. On El Salvador see Gerardo L. Munck, "Beyond Electoralism in El Salvador: Conflict Resolution through Negotiated Compromise," *Third World Quarterly*, vol. 14 (January 1993), pp. 75–93; and Patricia Weiss Fagen, "El Salvador: Lessons in Peace Consolidation," in Tom Farer, ed., *Beyond Sovereignty: Collectively Defending Democracy in the Americas* (Johns Hopkins University Press, 1996), pp. 213–37. On Mozambique see Chris Alden, "The UN and the Resolution of Conflict in Mozambique," *Journal of Modern African Studies*, vol. 3 (March 1995), pp. 103–08; and Richard Synge, *Mozambique: UN Peacekeeping in Action, 1992–94* (United States Institute of Peace, 1997). On Cambodia see Janet E. Heininger, *Peacekeeping in Transition: The United Nations in Cambodia* (New York: The Twentieth Century Fund Press, 1994); Trevor Findlay, *Cambodia: The Legacy and Lessons of UNTAC*, SIPRI Research Report No. 9 (Oxford University Press, 1995); and Steven R. Ratner, "The United Nations in Cambodia: A Model for Resolution of Internal Conflicts?" in Lori Fisler Damrosch, ed., *Enforcing Restraint: Collective Intervention in Internal Conflicts* (New York: Council on Foreign Relations, 1993), pp. 241–73. On Angola see Margaret Joan Anstee, *Orphan of the Cold War: The Inside Story of the Collapse of the Angolan Peace Process* (St. Martin's Press, 1996). For recent analysis on Bosnia see Paul Shoup, "The Elections in Bosnia and Herzegovina: The End of an Illusion," *Problems of Post-Communism*, vol. 44 (January–February 1997), pp. 3–14.

6. Two international observer missions issued substantive reports. See Friends of Liberia, *Observation of 1997 Election: Republic of Liberia* (Rosslyn, Va., August 1997); and The Carter Center, *Observing the 1997 Special Elections Process in Liberia* (Atlanta, Ga., 1998). For earlier versions of some of the analysis included in this study see Terrence Lyons, "Peace and Elections in Liberia," in Krishna Kumar, ed., *Postconflict Elections, Democratization, and International Assistance* (Lynne Rienner, 1998); and Terrence Lyons, "Liberia's Path from Anarchy to Elections," *Current History*, vol. 97 (May 1998), pp. 229–33.

7. Rafael López-Pintor, "Reconciliation Elections: A Post-Cold War Experience," in Krishna Kumar, ed., *Rebuilding Societies after Civil War: Critical Roles for International Assistance* (Lynne Rienner, 1997); Krishna Kumar, ed., *Postconflict Elections, Democratization, and International Assistance* (Lynne Rienner, 1998); and Timothy D. Sisk and Andrew Reynolds, eds., *Elections and Conflict Management in Africa* (Washington: United States Institute of Peace, 1998).

8. For examples, see I. William Zartman, *Ripe for Resolution: Conflict and Intervention in Africa* (Oxford University Press, 1985); I. William Zartman, ed., *Elusive Peace: Negotiating an End to Civil Wars* (Brookings, 1995); Richard N. Haass, *Conflicts Unending: The United States and Regional Disputes* (Yale University Press, 1990); and Fen Osler Hampson, *Nurturing Peace: Why Peace Settlements Succeed or Fail* (Washington: United States

Institute of Peace, 1996). For some thoughts on implementing agreements in Africa, see Donald Rothchild, *Managing Ethnic Conflict in Africa: Pressures and Incentives for Cooperation* (Brookings, 1997), pp. 273–77.

9. For a classic study, see Guillermo O'Donnell and Philippe Schmitter, *Transitions from Authoritarian Rule: Tentative Conclusions about Uncertain Democracies* (Johns Hopkins University Press, 1986). For analysis on Africa, see Michael Bratton and Nicolas van de Walle, *Democratic Experiments in Africa: Regime Transitions in Comparative Perspective* (Cambridge University Press, 1997). Yossi Shain and Juan J. Linz, *Between States: Interim Governments and Democratic Transitions* (Cambridge University Press, 1995), p. 4, suggest that "the type of interim administration is crucial in determining the subsequent regime."

10. Stephan Haggard and Steven B. Webb, eds., *Voting for Reform: Democracy, Political Liberalization, and Economic Adjustment* (Oxford University Press, 1994); and Adam Przeworski, *Democracy and the Market: Political and Economic Reforms in Eastern Europe and Latin America* (Cambridge University Press, 1991).

11. I thank Susan Woodward for making this point to me in the context of the Balkans.

12. Stephen John Stedman, *Peacemaking in Civil War: International Mediation in Zimbabwe, 1974–1980* (Lynne Rienner, 1991), p. 9. See also Roy Licklider, "The Consequences of Negotiated Settlements in Civil Wars, 1945–1993," *American Political Science Review*, vol. 89 (September 1995), pp. 685–87; Paul R. Pillar, *Negotiating Peace: War Termination as a Bargaining Process* (Princeton University Press, 1983), pp. 24–25; and Barbara F. Walter, "The Critical Barrier to Civil War Settlement," *International Organization*, vol. 51 (Summer 1997), p. 335.

13. I. William Zartman, "Dynamics and Constraints in Negotiations in Internal Conflicts," in Zartman, ed., *Elusive Peace*, p. 3.

14. Charles King, *Ending Civil Wars*, International Institute for Strategic Studies, Adelphi Paper 30 (Oxford University Press, 1997), p. 13.

15. Zartman, *Ripe for Resolution*; Haass, *Conflicts Unending*; Stedman, *Peacemaking in Civil War*; and Hampson, *Nurturing Peace*, pp. 13–16, 210–14. For a practitioner's account, see Chester Crocker, *High Noon in Southern Africa: Making Peace in a Rough Neighborhood* (Norton, 1993).

16. See Roy Licklider, "What Have We Learned and Where Do We Go from Here?" in Licklider, ed., *Stopping the Killing*, p. 309.

17. Zartman, "Dynamics and Constraints in Negotiations in Internal Conflicts," pp. 20–21; and Rothchild, *Managing Ethnic Conflict in Africa*, pp. 243–80.

18. Hampson, *Nurturing Peace*, p. 3. See also Chester A. Crocker and Fen Osler Hampson, "Making Peace Settlements Work," *Foreign Policy*, no. 104 (Fall 1996), p. 55.

19. Stephen John Stedman, "Negotiation and Mediation in Internal Conflict," in Michael E. Brown, ed., *The International Dimensions of Internal Conflicts* (MIT Press, 1996), pp. 366–67.

20. Gérald Prunier, *The Rwanda Crisis: History of a Genocide* (Columbia University Press, 1995), pp. 213–80. The Rwanda Patriotic Front government that came to power after the genocide, however, continually refers to the Arusha Accords as the framework that legitimizes its government.

21. Shain and Linz, *Between States*, pp. 3–21.

22. Timothy D. Sisk, *Democratization in South Africa: The Elusive Social Contract* (Princeton University Press, 1995); and Vincent T. Maphai, "A Season for Power-Sharing," *Journal of Democracy*, vol. 7 (January 1996), pp. 67–81.

23. On pacts see Terry Lynn Karl, "Dilemmas of Democratization in Latin America," *Comparative Politics*, vol. 23 (October 1990), pp. 1–21; Guillermo O'Donnell and Philippe Schmitter, *Transitions from Authoritarian Rule: Tentative Conclusions about Uncertain Democracies* (Johns Hopkins University Press, 1986), pp. 37–47; and Giuseppe Di Palma, *To Craft Democracies: An Essay on Democratic Transitions* (University of California Press, 1990), pp. 86–90.

24. Marina Ottaway, "Democratization in Collapsed States," in I. William Zartman, ed., *Collapsed States: The Disintegration and Restoration of Legitimate Authority* (Boulder, Colo.: Lynne Rienner, 1995), p. 248.

25. Donald Rothchild, "Bargaining and State Breakdown in Africa," *Nationalism and Ethnic Politics*, vol. 1 (Spring 1995), pp. 54–72.

26. Richard Synge, *Mozambique: UN Peacekeeping in Action, 1992–1994* (Washington: United States Institute of Peace, 1997), p. 52.

27. David Holiday and William Stanley, "Building the Peace: Preliminary Lessons from El Salvador," *Journal of International Affairs*, vol. 46 (Winter 1993), pp. 427–30.

28. Interview with representative of international human rights organization in Ian Johnstone, *Rights and Reconciliation: UN Strategies in El Salvador,* International Peace Academy Occasional Paper Series (Boulder, Colo.: Lynne Rienner, 1995), p. 55.

29. Kimberly Mahling Clark, *Mozambique's Transition from War to Peace: USAID's Lessons Learned* (Research and Reference Services, United States Agency for International Development, Center for Development Information and Evaluation, April 1996), p. 3.

30. Margaret Joan Anstee, *Orphan of the Cold War: The Inside Story of the Collapse of the Angolan Peace Process, 1992–93* (St. Martin's, 1996).

31. For a discussion of the security dilemma in internal conflicts, see Barry R. Posen, "The Security Dilemma and Ethnic Conflict," in Michael E. Brown, ed., *Ethnic Conflict and International Security* (Princeton University Press, 1993), pp. 103–24; and David A. Lake and Donald Rothchild, "Containing Fear: The Origins and Management of Ethnic Conflict," *International Security*, vol. 21 (Fall 1996), pp. 41–75.

32. Stedman, "Negotiation and Mediation in Internal Conflict," p. 365; and Charles King, *Ending Civil Wars*, International Institute for Strategic Studies Adelphi Paper 308 (Oxford University Press, 1997), pp. 50–52.

33. Stephen John Stedman, "Spoiler Problems in Peace Processes," *International Security*, vol. 22 (Fall 1997), p. 5.

34. Barbara F. Walter, "The Critical Barrier to Civil War Settlement," *International Organization*, vol. 51 (Summer 1997), pp. 335–36.

35. Brian Hall, "Blue Helmets, Empty Guns," *New York Times Sunday Magazine*, January 2, 1994, p. 24.

36. Adam Przeworski, "Democracy as a Contingent Outcome of Conflicts," in Jon Elster and Rune Slagstad, eds., *Constitutionalism and Democracy* (Cambridge University Press, 1988), p. 62.

37. I first heard this characterization from Tom Farer at a U.S. Agency for International Development conference, "Promoting Democracy, Human Rights, and Reintegration in Post-conflict Societies," Washington, D.C., October 30–31, 1997.

38. Timothy D. Sisk, *Power Sharing and International Mediation in Ethnic Conflict* (Washington: United States Institute of Peace, 1996), pp. 115, 85.

39. Stephen John Stedman, "UN Intervention in Civil Wars: Imperatives of Choice and Strategy," in Donald C. F. Daniel and Bradd C. Hayes, eds., *Beyond Traditional Peacekeeping* (St. Martin's, 1995), p. 57.

40. Marina Ottaway, "Liberation Movements and Transition to Democracy: The Case of the A.N.C.," *Journal of Modern African Studies*, vol. 29 (March 1991), pp. 61–82.

41. Nat J. Colletta, Markus Kostner, and Ingo Wiederhofer, *The Transition from War to Peace in Sub-Saharan Africa* (World Bank, 1996). See also Nicole Ball, "Demobilizing and Reintegrating Soldiers: Lessons from Africa," in Kumar, ed., *Rebuilding Societies after Civil War*, chap. 4; and Kees Kingma, "Demobilization of Combatants after Civil Wars in Africa and their Reintegration into Civilian Life," *Policy Sciences*, vol. 30 (August 1997), pp. 151–65.

42. Gerardo L. Munck, "Beyond Electoralism in El Salvador: Conflict Resolution through Negotiated Compromise," *Third World Quarterly*, vol. 14 (January 1993), p. 87. For analysis on the problem of guerillas and elections in Colombia and elsewhere in Latin America, see Matthew Soberg Shugart, "Guerrillas and Elections: An Institutionalist Perspective on the Costs of Conflict and Competition," *International Studies Quarterly*, vol. 36 (June 1992), pp. 121–52.

43. S/26005, June 29, 1993, para. 11. See Johnstone, *Rights and Reconciliation*, p. 51.

44. Synge, *Mozambique*, p. 35. For analysis on the transformation of Renamo, see Carrie Manning, "Constructing Opposition in Mozambique: Renamo as Political Party," *Journal of Southern African Studies*, vol. 24 (March 1998), pp. 161–90.

45. Terrence Lyons, "Closing the Transition: The May 1996 Elections in Ethiopia," *Journal of Modern African Studies*, vol. 34 (March 1996), pp. 121–42.

46. Roberta Cohen and Francis M. Deng, *Masses in Flight: The Global Crisis of Internal Displacement* (Brookings, 1998), pp. 291–303.

47. Some of my thoughts on the importance of time in political transitions were developed in analyzing the Somalia intervention. See Ken Menkhaus and Terrence Lyons, "What Are the Lessons to Be Learned from Somalia?" *CSIS Africa Notes* no. 144 (January 1993), p. 8; and Terrence Lyons and Ahmed I. Samatar, *Somalia: State Collapse, Multilateral Intervention, and Strategies for Political Reconstruction* (Brookings, 1995), p. 74.

48. David Hirschmann, "Improving Crisis Management in the Imperfect World of Foreign Electoral Assistance," *Public Administration and Development*, vol. 18 (January 1998), pp. 23–36.

49. See Susan L. Woodward, "Statement to the Senate Foreign Relations Committee," Hearings on the Midterm Assessment of the Dayton Accords in Bosnia and Herzegovina, September 10, 1996.

CHAPTER 2

1. ECOWAS consists of Benin, Burkina Faso, Cape Verde, Côte d'Ivoire, Gambia, Ghana, Guinea, Guinea-Bissau, Liberia, Mali, Mauritania, Niger, Nigeria, Senegal, Sierra Leone, and Togo.

2. Victor Tanner, "Liberia: Railroading Peace," *Review of African Political Economy*, vol. 25 (March 1998), pp. 133–147.

3. For background, see Martin Lowenkopf, "Liberia: Putting the State Back Together," in I. William Zartman, ed., *Collapsed States: The Disintegration and Restoration of Legitimate Authority* (Lynne Rienner, 1995); and Stephen Ellis, "Liberia 1989–1994: A Study of Ethnic and Spiritual Violence," *African Affairs*, vol. 94 (April 1995), pp. 165–97.

4. For an account of the humanitarian dimensions see Colin Scott, "Liberia: A Nation Displaced," in Roberta Cohen and Francis M. Deng, eds., *The Forsaken People: Case Studies of the Internally Displaced* (Brookings, 1998); and U.S. Committee for Refugees, *Uprooted Liberians: Casualties of a Brutal War* (Washington: U.S. Committee for Refugees, 1992).

5. J. Gus Liebenow, *Liberia: The Quest for Democracy* (Indiana University Press, 1987), pp. 135–39; and Christopher Clapham, *An Essay in Comparative Politics: Liberia and Sierra Leone* (Cambridge University Press, 1976). For a discussion of the role of ethnicity in Liberian politics see Eghosa E. Osaghe, *Ethnicity, Class and the Struggle for State Power in Liberia*, CODESRIA Monograph Series 1/96 (Dakar: Codesria, 1996).

6. These leaders continued to play major roles in the 1990s, Sawyer as president of the Interim Government of National Unity, Tipoteh, Fahnbulleh, and Matthews as presidential candidates in July 1997.

7. For an analytical account of these events see Jimmy D. Kandeh, "What Does the 'Militariat' Do When it Rules? Military Regimes: The Gambia, Sierra Leone, and Liberia," *Review of African Political Economy*, vol. 23 (September 1996), pp. 387–404.

8. Liebenow, *Liberia: The Quest for Democracy*, pp. 280–96. In a statement that Liberians remembered in 1997, then Assistant Secretary of State for

African Affairs Chester Crocker made the following astonishing remark: "The prospects for national reconciliation were brightened by Doe's claim that he won only a narrow 51 percent election victory." "Liberia and the United States Policy," Hearing before the Subcommittee on African Affairs of the Senate Committee on Foreign Relations, 99th Cong. 1 sess. (Government Printing Office, 1985), p. 2.

9. International Human Rights Law Group, "Statement on Liberia's Elections," in "Liberia and the United States Policy," Hearing before the Subcommittee on African Affairs of the Senate Committee on Foreign Relations, 99th Cong. 1 sess. (Government Printing Office, 1985), pp. 50–52.

10. Lawyers Committee for Human Rights, *Liberia: A Promise Betrayed* (New York, 1986). See also Stephen Ellis, "Liberia, 1989–1994: A Study of Ethnic and Spiritual Violence," *African Affairs*, vol. 94 (April 1995), pp. 178–80.

11. See Reed Kramer, "Liberia: Casualty of the Cold War?" *CSIS Africa Notes*, no. 174 (July 1995), pp. 5–7.

12. Kenneth L. Brown, "Mediation by Influence: American Policy toward the Liberian War," Ph.D. dissertation, University of Cape Coast, 1995.

13. Africa Watch, *Liberia: Flight from Terror* (New York, 1991).

14. The embassy facilitated the granting of visas to some of Doe's most ruthless supporters, including Edward Smith and Charles Julu, in the hope of encouraging the collapse of Doe's hold on power. Doe, however, continued to make unrealistic demands in return for accepting exile, including a scholarship at an Ivy League university in the United States. For details see Brown, "Mediation by Influence," p. 102; and Bill Berkeley, "Out of Africa: Liberian War Criminals in America," *New Republic*, April 6, 1994, pp. 12–14.

15. Veronica Nmoma, "The Civil Crisis in Liberia: An American Response," *Journal of African Policy Studies*, vol. 1 (June 1995), pp. 63–84. The later U.S. intervention in Somalia, however, raised the question of whether this support would last.

16. ICRC Report, "Liberia: Terrible Human Tragedy, 1990," in M. Weller, ed., *Regional Peace-Keeping and International Enforcement: The Liberian Crisis* (Cambridge University Press, 1984), pp. 123–24.

17. On ECOMOG see Robert A. Mortimer, "ECOMOG, Liberia, and Regional Security in West Africa," and Margaret Aderinsola Vogt, "The Involvement of ECOWAS in Liberia's Peacekeeping," in Edmond J. Keller and Donald Rothchild, eds., *Africa in the New International Order: Rethinking State Sovereignty and Regional Security* (Lynne Rienner, 1996), chaps. 11 and 12; George Klay Kieh Jr., "The Obstacles to the Peaceful Resolution of the Liberian Civil Conflict," *Studies in Conflict and Terrorism*, vol. 17 (January–March 1994), pp. 97–108; Ademola Adeleke, "The Politics and Diplomacy of Peacekeeping in West Africa: The ECOWAS Operation in Liberia," *Journal of Modern African Studies*, vol. 33 (December 1995), pp. 569–93; Clement E. Adibe, "The Liberian Conflict and the ECOWAS–UN Partnership," *Third World Quarterly*, vol. 18 (July 1997), pp. 471–88; Herbert Howe, "Lessons of Liberia: ECOMOG and Regional Peacekeeping,"

International Security, vol. 21 (Winter 1996–1997), pp. 145–76. Relevant materials and ECOWAS declarations are included in Weller, *Regional Peace-Keeping and International Enforcement*.

18. David Wippman, "Enforcing the Peace: ECOWAS and the Liberian Civil War," in Lori Fisler Damrosch, ed., *Enforcing Restraint: Collective Intervention in Internal Conflicts* (New York: Council on Foreign Relations, 1993), p. 165. The United Nations did not take up the question of Liberia until January 1991 when it passed a resolution that commended the efforts of ECOWAS and called on all parties to respect the Bamako cease-fire. See Statement by the President, "The Situation in Liberia," S/22133, January 22, 1991, reprinted in United Nations Department of Public Information, *The United Nations and the Situation in Liberia*, Reference Paper (New York, February 1997), p. 36.

19. "ECOWAS Standing Mediation Committee, Banjul, Republic of Gambia, Final Communiqué of the First Session, 7 August 1990," reprinted in Weller, *Regional Peace-Keeping and International Enforcement*, p. 74.

20. ECOWAS, Decision A/DEC.1/8/90, article II, para. 4, reprinted in Weller, *Regional Peace-Keeping and International Enforcement*, p. 68.

21. *West Africa*, August 6–12, 1990, p. 2236. Taylor, upon hearing reports of the planned ECOWAS intervention, appealed for a general mobilization "in order to fight any foreign intervention." Cited in BBC Monitoring Report, August 5, 1990, reprinted in Weller, *Regional Peace-Keeping and International Enforcement*, p. 63.

22. BBC Monitoring Report, August 27, 1990, in Weller, *Regional Peace-Keeping and International Enforcement*, p. 87.

23. Tunji Lardner, Jr., "Liberia: An African Tragedy," *Africa Report*, vol. 35 (November–December 1990), pp. 13–16. Video tapes of Prince Johnson torturing Doe before killing him circulated widely across West Africa. Johnson eventually left Liberia and became a "born again" minister in Nigeria. See AFP, "Former Liberian Rebel Leader Who Murdered Doe Is 'Born Again,'" April 7, 1997.

24. Mark Huband, "Liberia: The Power Vacuum," *Africa Report*, vol. 36 (January–February 1991), pp. 27–30.

25. Reed Kramer, "Liberia: Casualty of the Cold War's End?" *CSIS Africa Notes*, no. 174 (July 1995), p. 1.

26. An NGO press officer cited in Colin Scott, *Humanitarian Action and Security in Liberia, 1989–1994*, Occasional Paper 20 (Providence, R.I.: Thomas J. Watson Jr. Institute for International Studies, 1995), p. 9.

27. Scott, *Humanitarian Action and Security in Liberia*, p. x. This study contains a number of insights on the impossibility of conducting apolitical humanitarian operations during internal war.

28. Quoted in Reed Kramer, "Liberia: Casualty of the Cold War?" *CSIS Africa Notes*, no. 174, (July 1995), p. 2.

29. The texts of these agreements along with background and analysis are included in Jeremy Armon and Andy Carl, eds., *Accord: The Liberian Peace Process, 1990–1996* (London: Conciliation Resources, 1996).

30. "Interview: Patrick Seyon, Liberian Electoral Commission Co-Chairman," *Africa Report*, vol. 37 (March-April 1992), p. 6.

31. Howe, "Lessons of Liberia," p. 156; and "Liberia: Wild Cards in the Pack," *Africa Confidential*, vol. 32 (November 22, 1991), pp. 6–7.

32. Stephen Riley and Max Sesay, "Liberia: After Abuja," *Review of African Political Economy*, vol. 23 (September 1996), p. 430; Max Ahmadu Sesay, "Politics and Society in Post-War Liberia," *Journal of Modern African Studies*, vol. 34 (September 1996), p. 397; and "Liberia: Wild Cards in the Pack," *Africa Confidential*, vol. 32 (November 22, 1991), pp. 6–7.

33. William Reno, "The Business of War in Liberia," *Current History*, vol. 95 (May 1996), pp. 212–13; William Reno, "Reinvention of an African Patrimonial State: Charles Taylor's Liberia," *Third World Quarterly*, vol. 16 (January 1995), pp. 109–20. For a profile of Taylor during this period see Kenneth Noble, "In Liberia's Illusory Peace, Rebel Leader Rules Empire of His Own Design," *New York Times*, April 14, 1992, p. A3.

34. Peter Da Costa, "Liberia: Peace Postponed," *Africa Report*, vol. 37 (May–June 1992), p. 52.

35. Stephen Ellis, "Liberia 1989–1994: A Study of Ethnic and Spiritual Violence," *African Affairs*, vol. 94 (April 1995), p. 185.

36. William Reno, "The Business of War in Liberia," *Current History*, vol. 95 (May 1996), p. 211. See also Quentin Outram, "'It's Terminal Either Way: An Analysis of Armed Conflict in Liberia, 1989–1996," *Review of African Political Economy*, vol. 24 (September 1997), pp. 355–71.

37. For a sample of Western reporting on the violence see Thomas Friedman, "Heart of Darkness," *New York Times*, January 21, 1996, p. E15; Michel Galy, "Drôle de Paix," *Le Monde Diplomatique*, January 1996, p. 26; Cindy Shiner, "In Battle and in Politics, Liberia's Motley Factions Fight On," *Washington Post*, August 7, 1994, p. A27. Friedman describes Liberia as "a country in meltdown . . . an African 'Clockwork Orange' in which militias don't even pretend to stand for anything" and described Taylor and Kromah as "peacocks strutting through the graveyard, killers with fax machines." For a scholarly discussion of the nature of the violence see Stephen Ellis, "Liberia 1989–1994: A Study of Ethnic and Spiritual Violence," *African Affairs*, vol. 94 (April 1995), pp.165–97. On child soldiers see Human Rights Watch, *Easy Prey: Child Soldiers in Liberia* (New York, 1994); and Jonathan C. Randal, "No Child's Play for Boy Soldiers: Liberia's Young Warriors Are Steeled by Combat, Witch Doctors," *Washington Post*, June 12, 1995, p. A12.

38. Keith B. Richburg, "Liberia's Surreal Civil War," *Washington Post*, November 15, 1992, p. A1.

39. United Nations, "Results of an Investigation by the Panel of Inquiry Appointed by the Secretary General into the Massacre near Harbel, Liberia, on the Night of June 5/6, 1993," New York, September 10, 1993. See Weller, *Regional Peace-Keeping and International Enforcement*, pp. 300–01. According to the UN high commissioner for refugees representative in Liberia: "The scene [in Harbel] was horrific. It was really a sight that no horror film or novel could match. It was unspeakable, just incomprehensible. . . . When you look

at it, you wonder whether these people were out of their minds." Cited in Peter da Costa, "Liberia: A[nother] Plan for Peace," *Africa Report*, vol. 38 (September–October 1993), p. 21.

40. Senegalese participation was important because it dampened the perception that ECOMOG was dominated by Anglophone states. Robert A. Mortimer, "Senegal's Rôle in ECOMOG: The Francophone Dimension in the Liberian Crisis," *Journal of Modern African Studies*, vol. 34 (June 1996), pp. 293–306.

41. "Liberia: Another Bend in the Road," *Africa Confidential*, vol. 33 (June 5, 1992), pp. 4–6; and Mortimer, "Senegal's Rôle in ECOMOG," p. 300.

42. Agence France-Presse, August 14, 1992, in Weller, *Regional Peace-Keeping and International Enforcement*, p. 207.

43. Final Communiqué of the Fifteenth Session of the Heads of State and Government of the Economic Community of West African States, Dakar, Senegal, July 27–29, 1992, reprinted in Weller, ed., *Regional Peace-Keeping and International Enforcement*, pp. 204–06.

44. Howe, "Lessons of Liberia," p. 158.

45. For analysis of an analogous situation with regard to peace talks in Ethiopia see Marina Ottaway, "Eritrea and Ethiopia: Negotiations in a Transitional Conflict," in I. William Zartman, ed., *Elusive Peace: Negotiating an End to Civil Wars* (Brookings, 1995), pp.103–19.

46. Radio ELBC interview with Taylor, October 26, 1992, reprinted in Weller, *Regional Peace-Keeping and International Enforcement*, p. 232.

47. Robert D. McFadden, "Five U.S. Nuns Are Shot to Death while Trapped by Liberian War," *New York Times*, November 1, 1992, p. A1.

48. Kenneth B. Noble, "Intensified Liberia War Threatens to Engulf Other African Nations," *New York Times*, November 15, 1992, p. A1.

49. Janet Fleishman, "Liberia: An Uncivil War," *Africa Report*, vol. 38 (May–June 1993), p. 58.

50. Howe, "Lessons of Liberia," p. 161; and Stephen P. Riley, "Intervention in Liberia: Too Little, Too Partisan," *World Today*, vol. 49 (March 1993), pp. 42–43.

51. Steven A. Holmes, "U.S. Tries to Blunt Harm of Remark on Liberian Peacekeepers," *New York Times*, November 15, 1992, p. A12. Cohen said the remark was "a slip of the tongue."

52. Africa Watch, *Waging War to Keep the Peace: The ECOMOG Intervention and Human Rights* (New York: Human Rights Watch, 1993).

53. The quote is from leaked State Department documents cited in Peter da Costa, "Liberia: Talking Tough to Taylor," *Africa Report*, vol. 38 (January-February 1993), p. 21; and "Liberia: Listening in to Washington," *Africa Confidential* , vol. 33 (November 20, 1992), p. 6.

54. S/RES/788 (November 19, 1992) in United Nations Department of Public Information, *The United Nations and the Situation in Liberia*, pp. 36–38. Since the embargo explicitly permitted weapons to be delivered to ECOMOG, the resolution was aimed at Taylor.

55. Melvis Dzisah, "West Africa-Politics: Dangerous Neighbours," Inter-Press Service (IPS), March 22, 1996. Libya also supported Taylor.

56. In Liberia, some referred to ECOMOG as Every Car and Moving Object Gone.

57. William Reno, "The Business of War in Liberia," *Current History*, vol. 94 (May 1996), pp. 214–15.

58. Steven A. Holmes, "Rebels in Liberia Reported to Suffer Setbacks," *New York Times*, March 11, 1993, p. A10; and Cindy Shiner, "As Accord Brings Peace, Liberians Try to Put Turbulent Past Behind Them," *Washington Post*, November 3, 1993, p. A19.

59. "Liberia: The Battle for Gbarnga," *Africa Confidential*, vol. 34 (May 28, 1993), p. 1. See also Mark Huband, "Targeting Taylor," *Africa Report*, vol. 38 (July-August 1993), pp. 29–32.

60. Karl Maier, "Air Raids on Liberia Intensify: Civilians Flee Strikes by W. African Force," *Washington Post*, April 4, 1993, p. A40.

61. Ben Asante, "Peace Looms in Liberia," *West Africa*, July 26–August 1, 1993, pp. 1292–94; and Peter Da Costa, "A[nother] Plan for Peace," *Africa Report*, vol. 38 (September–October 1993), pp. 20–23.

62. S/RES/866 (September 22, 1993) in Weller, *Regional Peace-Keeping and International Enforcement*, pp. 412–14.

63. Report of the Secretary-General on Liberia, S/26422, September 9, 1993, para. 13, reprinted in Weller, *Regional Peace-Keeping and International Enforcement*, p. 376. See also Clement E. Adibe, "The Liberian Conflict and the ECOWAS-UN Partnership," *Third World Quarterly*, vol. 18 (July 1997), pp. 471–88, for a good analysis of the UNOMIL-ECOMOG relationship.

64. UNOMIL reached a peak of 374 military observers and military support personnel in February 1994. See United Nations Department of Public Information, *The United Nations and the Situation in Liberia*.

65. Cindy Shiner, "Liberian Government Sworn in: Peacekeepers Begin Collecting Weapons," *Washington Post*, March 8, 1994, p. A13.

66. Howe, "Lessons of Liberia," p. 169.

67. Kenneth B. Noble, "As Liberia's Factions Talk, Strife and Fear Drag on," *New York Times*, November 5, 1993, p. A3.

68. Stephen Ellis, "Liberia 1989–1994: A Study of Ethnic and Spiritual Violence," *African Affairs* vol. 94 (April 1995), pp. 173–74; and Janet Fleishman, "Liberia: An Uncivil War," *Africa Report*, vol. 38 (May–June 1993), pp. 56–59.

69. "Sierra Leone: The Threat from the East," *Africa Confidential*, vol. 35 (April 1, 1994), pp. 6–7.

70. "Fighting Flares in Liberia Despite Two-Day-Old Cease-Fire Accord," *Washington Post*, September 15, 1994, p. A33. On September 9, forty-three UNOMIL and six NGO workers at nine sites across northern and eastern Liberia were detained by the NPFL and had their communication and transportation equipment seized in an effort by Taylor's fighters to improve their logistical capacity. See United Nations Department of Public Information, *The*

United Nations and the Situation in Liberia (New York, February 1997), p. 10. Several of the observers were beaten before they were eventually released.

71. Cindy Shiner, "Peacekeepers Put Down Liberia Coup," *Washington Post*, September 16, 1994, p. A33. Cindy Shiner, "Liberia: The Authority Vacuum," *Africa Report*, vol. 39 (November–December 1994), p. 23, described the Julu coup as "one of the most ridiculous rebellions in modern African history." For more on Julu and the story of his earlier exile in the United States see Bill Berkeley, "Out of Africa: Liberian War Criminals in America," *New Republic*, vol. 206 (April 6, 1994), pp. 12–14.

72. For a journalist's account of the exasperation and despair of late 1994, see Howard W. French, "As War Factions Shatter, Liberia Falls into Chaos," *New York Times*, October 22, 1994, p. A4.

73. *West Africa* stated, for example, "It is not clear what made (UNSGSR) Mr. Gordon-Somers make such dedicated effort to rescue the warlords from their dilemma of loss of authority." "Liberia: Old Issues, New Problems," *West Africa*, September 26, 1994. See also Max Ahmadu Sesay, "Politics and Society in Post-War Liberia," *Journal of Modern African Studies*, vol. 34 (September 1996), p. 399. For an excellent analysis of the Liberian peace process up to the Akosombo Agreement, see Richard Carver, "Liberia: What Hope for Peace?" (WRITENET, October 1994).

74. Jonathan C. Randal, "Liberia's Chronic Civil War Threatens to Burst Its Borders," *Washington Post*, June 12, 1995, p. A12. "Trekking to Monrovia," *Africa Confidential* (July 21, 1995), pp. 3–4.

75. In a telling indication of the complexity of the peace process, the Abuja Accord was technically called an amendment and supplement to the Cotonou Accord, the Akosombo Agreement and its Accra Clarification.

76. Adekeye Adebajo, "Dog Days in Monrovia," *West Africa*, (April 22–28, 1996), pp. 622–23.

77. Stephen Buckley, "Liberia Tries Peace after 5-Year Civil War," *Washington Post*, September 10, 1995, p. A28. See also Washington Office on Africa, "Liberia: More U.S. Support Needed," *Washington Notes on Africa Update*, October 22, 1995.

78. See S/1042, "Fourteenth Progress Report of the Secretary-General on the United Nations Observer Mission in Liberia," December 18, 1995, and S/47, "Fifteenth Progress Report of the Secretary-General on the United Nations Observer Mission in Liberia," January 23, 1996.

79. Melvis Dzisah, "Liberia-Politics: Back in the Emergency Ward," Inter-Press Service, January 11, 1996.

80. Howard W. French, "Peace Plan for Liberia Seeks to Demilitarize the Capital," *New York Times*, May 9, 1996, p. A3. See also William Reno, "The Business of War in Liberia," *Current History*, vol. 95 (May 1996), p. 215.

81. See the comments by former Finance Minister Wilson Tarpeh in Howard W. French, "After Years of War, A Lawless Liberia," *New York Times*, February 1, 1996, p. A9.

82. Stephen Riley and Max Sesay, "Liberia: After Abuja," *Review of African Political Economy*, vol. 23 (September 1996), p. 434.

83. Max Ahmadu Sesay, "Politics and Society in Post-War Liberia," *Journal of Modern African Studies*, vol. 34 (September 1996), pp. 402–04.

84. Howard W. French, "Key Ally Gone, Liberia Leader Vows to Fight," *New York Times*, May 3, 1996, p. A10.

85. "Liberia: Out of Control," *Africa Confidential* 37 (May 10, 1996), p. 1. For an account of the fighting see Jonathan C. Randal, "In Liberia's Mean Streets, Chaos Is King," *Washington Post*, April 18, 1996, p. A1.

86. Report of the Secretary-General, "Assistance for the Rehabilitation and Reconstruction of Liberia," United Nations, A/51/303, August 23, 1996, para. 17. UN officials reported a "frenzy of looting" on April 11 and "absolute anarchy in the streets" on April 12. See "Dispatches from the Front," *UN Chronicle*, no. 2 (1996), pp. 12–13.

87. Howard W. French, "Ledger for Liberia's War: Profit(eering) and Loss," *New York Times* April 30, 1996, p. A8; and "Liberia: Out of Control," *Africa Confidential*, p. 1.

88. See the report by Samuel Kofi Woods, director, Catholic Justice and Peace Commission, "Briefing Paper on Liberia," September 11, 1996. Woods soon returned to Monrovia, where he continued to act as an advocate for human rights willing to challenge the factional leaders.

89. Quoted in Howard W. French, "U.S. Wins Liberians' Pledge to Back Truce," *New York Times*, April 26, 1996, p. A3.

90. Howard W. French, "Peace Plan for Liberia," p. A3.

91. Even within Liberia, however, the problem was often discussed in terms of the quality of leadership rather than institutions. See Max Ahmadu Sesay, "Politics and Society in Post-War Liberia," *Journal of Modern African Studies*, vol. 34 (September 1996), p. 413.

92. Howe, "Lessons of Liberia," p. 146.

93. Abacha quoted by Lagos Radio, "Nigeria Government Spends $3 Billion on Peace in Liberia," in Foreign Broadcast Information Service, August 3, 1997. The figure is, of course, impossible to confirm. Many observers believe that Nigeria, or at least prominent members of the military involved in Liberia, profited from the intervention by making deals with factional leaders and engaging in trade of looted materials.

94. For a critique of the failure of the United States and the United Nations to link force and a political strategy in Somalia, see Terrence Lyons and Ahmed I. Samatar, *Somalia: State Collapse, Multilateral Intervention, and Strategies for Political Reconstruction* (Brookings, 1995), pp. 36–62.

95. Mortimer, "ECOMOG, Liberia, and Regional Security in West Africa," p. 149.

96. Stedman, "Conflict and Conciliation in Sub-Saharan Africa," p. 252.

CHAPTER 3

1. In addition to the sources cited, much of the information in this chapter is based on the author's observations and discussions in Liberia during March and April to August 1997, when he served as senior program adviser to

The Carter Center in Monrovia. The opinions are his own and do not reflect the positions of The Carter Center or its funders.

2. Quoted in Howard W. French, "In Liberia, Life Returns to a Grim Normality," *New York Times*, August 21, 1996, p. A8.

3. Associated Press, "New Interim Leader is Chosen for Liberia," *New York Times*, August 19, 1996, p. A4.

4. Panafrican News Agency, "Liberia: More West African Troops Set for Liberia," August 28, 1996. For a series of strongly pro-Nigerian accounts of ECOMOG in 1997 see Ben Asante, "The ECOMOG Miracle," "A No-Nonsense Commander," and Lindsay Barrett, "Nigeria's Pivotal Role," *West Africa*, March 24–30, 1997, pp. 462–69.

5. Violence along the border began to threaten stability in Côte d'Ivoire and thereby further encouraged authorities to clamp down on factional activities. See Melvis Dzisah, "West Africa–Politics: Dangerous Neighbors," Inter-Press Service, March 22, 1996.

6. Amnesty International, for example, reported that one person was beaten to death and four others tortured during a weapons search in Grand Cape Mount County. See Amnesty International, "Liberia: Culture of Impunity and Continuing Human Rights Abuses by Peace-Keepers Must End as New Democratic Era Dawns," news release, AF/34/02/97, May 29, 1997. www.amnesty.org/news/1997/13400297.htm

7. French, "In Liberia, Life Returns to a Grim Normality," p. A8.

8. United Nations Department of Public Information, *The United Nations and the Situation in Liberia*, Reference Paper (New York, February 1997), p. 24; and Adekeye Adebajo, "Liberia: Two Weddings and a Funeral," *West Africa* (January 6–12, 1997), pp. 22–23.

9. Reuter, "Liberia's Taylor Says He Was Ambushed by Gunmen," October 31, 1996. Several people were killed in the attack, but Taylor was not injured. Taylor accused rival Krahn militia leaders Boley and Johnson in the attack. See "Liberia: Shooting in the Mansion," *Africa Confidential*, November 15, 1996, p. 8; "Liberia: The 'Coup" That Failed," *West Africa*, November 18–24, 1996, pp. 1796–97. Reflecting the high level of suspicions and distrust, rumors in Monrovia suggested that dissidents within the NPFL or even Taylor himself may have been responsible.

10. See map at the front of the book.

11. The United States provided $40 million in nonlethal assistance to ECOMOG. See U.S. Agency for International Development, Bureau for Humanitarian Response, Office of Foreign Disaster Assistance, "Liberia—Complex Emergency," Fiscal Year 1997 Situation Report 1 (Washington, August 1997). The leased Russian helicopters, with Russian and Ukrainian pilots, and with American maintenance crews, carrying the insignias of the United States and ECOWAS, became a vivid symbol of the post–cold war order in West Africa as they flew Nigerian and other West African soldiers around Liberia.

12. Victor Tanner, "Liberia: Railroading Peace," *Review of African Political Economy*, vol. 25 (March 1998), pp. 133–47.

13. United Nations, "Twenty-Second Progress Report of the Secretary-General on the United Nations Observer Mission in Liberia," U.N. Doc. S/1997/237, March 19, 1997, para. 13; United Nations, "Final Report of the Secretary-General on the United Nations Observer Mission in Liberia," U.N. Doc. S/1997/712, September 12, 1997, para. 5. In some areas in the Southeast disarmament continued past the deadline into March. See Agence France-Presse, "Liberia-Disarmament: Disarmament Still Going on In Southeast," March 25, 1997.

14. Despite Kromah's clear violation of the Abuja Accord, ECOMOG allowed him to participate in the election after he apologized publicly. Agence France-Presse, "Kromah Apologizes for Hoarding Arms, Ammunition," March 14, 1997; and Paul Ejime, "ECOMOG Pardons Ex-Liberian Warlord," Panafrican News Agency, March 15, 1997. Weapons were also found in areas formerly under the control of Taylor, Boley, and Johnson.

15. Max Ahmadu Sesay, "Politics and Society in Post-War Liberia," Journal of Modern African Studies, vol. 34 (September 1996), pp. 405–09.

16. Friends of Liberia, "Liberia: Opportunities and Obstacles for Peace," December 1996, p. 5. See also The Carter Center, "Carter Center Liberia Pre-Election Mission: March 4–8, 1997," March 1997, p. 2. For comparative analysis of demobilization see Nat J. Colletta, Markus Kostner, and Ingo Wiederhofer, The Transition from War to Peace in Sub-Saharan Africa (Washington: World Bank, 1996); Nicole Ball, "Demobilizing and Reintegrating Soldiers: Lessons from Africa," in Krishna Kumar, ed., Rebuilding Societies after Civil War: Critical Roles for International Assistance (Lynne Rienner, 1997); and Kees Kingma, "Demobilization of Combatants after Civil Wars in Africa and their Reintegration into Civilian Life," Policy Sciences, vol. 30 (August 1997), pp. 151–65.

17. Victor Tanner, "Liberia: Railroading Peace," Review of African Political Economy, vol. 25 (March 1998), p. 137.

18. Refugee Policy Group, Participation of Refugees and Internally Displaced Persons in the Liberian Elections (Washington, March 1997); and Refugee Policy Group, Field Report: Refugee Repatriation and Electoral Participation in Liberia (Washington, June 1997).

19. See "A New Year–1997–Statement of the Alliance of Seven Political Parties," Monrovia, January 3, 1997.

20. For profiles see West Africa, July 14–20, 1997, pp. 1126–35.

21. William Reno, "The Business of War in Liberia," Current History, vol. 95 (May 1996), pp. 211–15.

22. "Twenty-First Progress Report of the Secretary-General on the United Nations Observer Mission in Liberia," S/1997/90, January 29, 1997, para. 21; and Ben Asante, "Liberia: Shifting to Top Gear," West Africa (February 24–March 2, 1997), p. 305.

23. The February ministerial meeting of the ECOWAS Committee of Nine made these decisions, which served as the mandate for the election commission. The committee, however, in a move emblematic of the manner in which decisions on the electoral process were made, never issued a formal commu-

niqué to reveal the results to the broader public. See International Foundation for Election Systems, "Liberia Project: Final Report."

24. Timothy D. Sisk, *Power Sharing and International Mediation in Ethnic Conflicts* (Washington: United States Institute of Peace, 1996), pp. 27–45; and International Institute for Democracy and Electoral Assistance, *The International IDEA Handbook of Electoral Design* (Stockholm, 1997).

25. "Twenty-Second Progress Report of the Secretary-General on the United Nations Observer Mission in Liberia," S/1997/237, March 19, 1997, para 20; James Butty, "The Electoral Process," *West Africa* (February 24–March 2, 1997), p. 307. Later surveys suggested that the 800,000 figure was exaggerated, particularly in Côte d'Ivoire. The 1998 United Nations Consolidated Inter-Agency Appeal for Liberia provided a figure of 480,000.

26. Refugee Policy Group, *Refugee Repatriation and Electoral Participation in Liberia* (Washington: Refugee Policy Group, June 1997).

27. Reuter, "Liberia Commission Installed to Run May 30 Polls," April 2, 1997.

28. "Liberia: Talking of Votes," *Africa Confidential*, vol. 38 (March 28, 1997), pp. 5–6.

29. Agence France-Presse, "Liberia Electoral Process in Question as Party Activity Suspended," April 23, 1997.

30. Agence France-Presse, "Only ECOWAS Can Change Elections Date: Ikimi," April 27, 1997.

31. "Twenty-Third Progress Report of the Secretary-General on the United Nations Observer Mission in Liberia," S/1997/478, June 19, 1997, para. 7.

32. Inter-Party Working Group, "Statement of Political Parties of the Republic of Liberia on the Prescribed Preconditions for the Holding of Free, Fair and Democratic Elections," May 1, 1997. The second Tuesday of October is election day under the Liberian constitution. The signatories consisted of the All-Liberia Coalition Party, Labor Party of Liberia, Liberia Action Party, Liberian National Union, Liberia People's Party, Liberia Unification Party, National Democratic Party of Liberia, People's Democratic Party of Liberia, Reformation Alliance of Liberia, True Whig Party, and Unity Party.

33. Paul Ejime, "Liberian Political Leaders Confer with Abacha," Pan-African News Agency, May 17, 1997; and Agence France-Presse, "Talks with Nigeria's Abacha on Liberian Election Open," May 16, 1997.

34. This date happened to be within two days of the statistically rainiest day in one of the world's wettest countries.

35. The original package included a plan for a centralized voting center in order to protect the secrecy of how communities voted. As in other elections in areas of conflict (Cambodia, parts of South Africa) some feared retaliation against entire villages if the vote was known. Memories of Doe's fraudulent manipulation of the vote counting at a centralized counting center in 1985, however, led most Liberians to favor counting at the voting site.

36. Among other things, the new budget deleted nearly the entire funding for civic education.

37. Attes Johnson, "Liberia-Politics: Voting for Real Peace," Inter-Press Service, July 2, 1997. Violence had earlier broken out in Gbarnga between Mandingos and ex-NPFL fighters. See Agence France-Presse, "Liberia: Security Tightened at Gbarnga after Lawless Acts," May 30, 1997.

38. "Liberia: Wooing Warriors," *Economist*, July 12, 1997, p. 40. See also Tina Susman, "Liberia Race between Woman, Warlord," Associated Press, July 18, 1997.

39. "Liberia: Not Charlie's Aunt," *Africa Confidential*, vol. 39 (June 20, 1997), pp. 5–6.

40. "Voter's Registration Starts, But . . ." *Transition* (Monrovia), June 27, 1997. Many election workers were transported to the wrong areas, including 300 who were sent by helicopter to Greenville in the far Southeast.

41. U.S. Agency for International Development, Bureau for Africa, "USAID Supports Liberia's Democratic Transition," *African Voices*, vol. 6 (Fall 1997), pp. 1, 6–7.

42. International Foundation for Elections Systems, "Liberia Project Final Report," draft.

43. Liberian Elections Observers Network (LEON), "LEON's Preliminary Statement," n.d.

44. The difficult conditions and lack of support to UNOMIL's field stations were particularly apparent. Several could only receive supplies by helicopter and lacked sufficient vehicles, fuel, and even food. The coup in Sierra Leone in May 1997 further complicated the difficult mission as large quantities of vehicles and other equipment destined for UNOMIL were looted.

45. One Liberian stated, "Of course I take rice from Taylor. After all, he stole it from us."

46. The IECOM has never released final figures on votes cast, making it impossible to provide a precise breakdown of the voting. Poorly designed tally sheets and confusing instructions made correlating specific ballot boxes to final results impossible.

47. July 19 was a very untypical bright and sunny day for that time of year in Liberia.

48. BBC, *Focus on Africa*, July 18, 1997, cited in Tanner, "Liberia: Railroading Peace."

49. Friends of Liberia, *Observation of 1997 Election*, pp. 32–33.

50. The Carter Center preliminary report noted that "in addition to providing security, some ECOMOG troops were involved in the conduct of the elections. In the future, it is important that the military's exclusive role should be to provide security, leaving the conduct of the elections to civilian election administrators." The Carter Center, "Liberian Special Elections Preliminary Statement," Monrovia, July 21, 1997.

51. "Twenty-Third Progress Report of the Secretary-General on the United Nations Observer Mission in Liberia," S/1997/478, June 19, 1997, paras. 20, 22.

52. The Carter Center, "Liberian Special Elections Preliminary Statement," July 21, 1997.

53. Friends of Liberia, *Observation of 1997 Election: Republic of Liberia* (Washington: Friends of Liberia, August 22, 1997), p. 1.

54. "Joint Certification Statement by the Chairman of ECOWAS and the Secretary General of the UN on the 1997 Liberian Special Elections," press release, July 24, 1997.

55. In one disturbing incident, Sirleaf's campaign manager, Dusty Wolokolie, was arrested by ECOMOG for alleging fraud. In their move to arrest Wolokolie, ECOMOG soldiers disrupted IECOM Chairman G. Henry Andrews's live radio broadcast of preliminary results. See John Chiahemen, "Taylor Ahead in Liberian Poll; Rival Protests," Reuters, July 21, 1997, and Donald G. McNeil, Jr., "Early Returns in Liberia Put Rebel Leader Far Ahead," *New York Times*, July 21, 1997.

56. James Butty, "Liberia: A Resounding Victory," *West Africa*, August 4-10, 1997, pp. 1252–53.

57. John Chiahemen, "Taylor Extends Lead in Liberian Election," Reuters, July 21, 1997.

58. In a complicated and poorly understood process, seats in the Senate and House of Representatives were "assigned" to geographic constituencies even though the election was conducted on the basis of a single, national constituency. The NPP, as the leading party, selected the seats it wished to fill, leaving the other parties with little choice. The result was that the Unity Party, ALCOP, the Alliance of Political Parties, LPP, and UPP could not put their strongest leaders into the legislature. The ALCOP and LPP initially refused to name their legislators as a result.

59. Others in attendance included the heads of state of Burkina Faso, Chad, Mali, Guinea, Guinea-Bissau, and Niger. Mangosuthu Buthelezi represented South Africa.

60. For an assessment by other international observers see Karen Lange (Friends of Liberia observer), "In Liberia, the People Choose an Awful Hope for Peace," *Washington Post*, August 10, 1997, p. C4; and Richard L. Sklar (UN observer), "From Bullets to Ballots in Liberia," *IGCC Newsletter*, vol. 13 (Fall 1997), pp. 5–7.

61. James Rupert, "Warlord Expected to Win National Vote in Liberia," *Washington Post*, July 21, 1997, p. A18.

62. Victor Tanner, "Liberia: Railroading Peace," *Review of African Political Economy*, vol. 25 (March 1998), p. 140.

63. Representative Donald Payne, who represented the United States at Taylor's inauguration, reportedly said that he believed Liberians "voted for stability. . . . By voting for Taylor they were making an investment in peace and security." Reported in Jim Fisher-Thompson, "Congressman Briefs President Clinton on Mission to Liberia," U.S. Information Agency, August 6, 1997.

64. On managing the spoiler problem, see Stephen John Stedman, "Negotiation and Mediation in Internal Conflict," in Michael E. Brown, ed., *The International Dimensions of Internal Conflict* (MIT Press, 1996), pp. 369–71.

65. James Rupert, "Liberians Voted for Warlord Despite Doubts," *Washington Post*, July 22, 1997, p. A17.

66. Sheikh Karfumba F. Konneh, "Peace and Democracy: The Road Ahead for Liberia," speech delivered at a workshop sponsored by the National Democratic Institute, Monrovia, August 1997.

67. Most observers believed the quick timetable favored Taylor. An alternative line of argument that seems just as credible is that Taylor was the only candidate with the resources and organizational structure to continue the campaign into the fall. Sirleaf and the other civilian candidates efforts' may have collapsed if the campaign had been extended.

CHAPTER 4

1. John Chiahemen, "Liberians Vote in Peace against War," Reuters, July 19, 1997. A number of Western journalists noted similar language. Another voter is quoted as saying, "Charles Taylor spoiled this country, so he's the best man to fix it." See Donald G. McNeil Jr., "Under Scrutiny, Postwar Liberia Goes to Polls," *New York Times*, July 20, 1997. Yet another voter is quoted as saying, "He killed my mother, and he killed my father and I don't care–I love Charles Ghankay Taylor." See Donald G. McNeil Jr., "Early Returns in Liberia Put Rebel Leader Far Ahead," *New York Times*, July 21, 1997.

2. A leading Liberian religious leader, Sheikh Konneh, for example, described the process as an exercise in "inalienable rights: the right to choose leaders." See Sheikh Kafumba F. Konneh, "Peace and Democracy: The Road Ahead for Liberia," speech delivered to workshop organized by the National Democratic Institute, Monrovia, August 1997.

3. For an analytical discussion of building peace and the importance of reconciliation and relationship building see John Paul Lederach, *Building Peace: Sustainable Reconciliation in Divided Societies* (U.S. Institute of Peace Press, 1997), especially pp. 23–37.

4. Agence France-Presse, "Liberia's Taylor Addresses Nation on State of Economy," August 21, 1997; "Final Report of the Secretary-General on the United Nations Observer Mission in Liberia," S/1997/712, September 12, 1997.

5. Remi Oyo, "Development-Liberia: A Tough Road from War to Peace," Inter-Press Service, December 3, 1997.

6. The U.S.-funded Star Radio was closed for a time in early January 1998. See Agence France-Presse, "Liberian Government Shuts Down Foreign-Run Radio Station," January 7, 1998.

7. Dokie, his wife, sister, and cousin were found near Gbarnga, decapitated and burned. He was arrested by Taylor's Special Security Service while traveling to a family wedding. See Agence France-Presse, "Liberian Police Arrest Four after Murder of Politician," December 10, 1997.

8. James Butty, "The Task of Economic Rebuilding," *West Africa* (November 24–30, 1997), p. 1839.

9. Agence France-Presse, "ECOMOG Chief Ends Liberia Tour with Regrets, Accusations," January 9, 1998; and "Liberian Daily News Bulletin," Star Radio, January 7, 1998.

10. Desmond Davies, "The Key to Security," West Africa (November 24–30, 1997), pp. 1840–41.

11. Jeff Cooper, "Politics-West Africa: ECOMOG Gets New Mandate in Liberia," Inter-Press Service, June 15, 1998.

12. George Gedda, "Once More, Liberia," WorldView, vol. 10 (Fall 1997), p. 73.

13. The relationship of the elections to other provisions of the Dayton Agreement, ranging from the arrest of war criminals to the reversal of ethnic cleansing, are yet another set of goals. For an evaluation of the 1996 Bosnian elections see International Crisis Group, Elections in Bosnia and Herzegovina (ICG Bosnia Project, September 22, 1996). www.intl-crisis-group.org/projects/bosnia/reports

14. See Jennifer McCoy, Larry Garber, and Robert Pastor, "Pollwatching and Peacemaking," Journal of Democracy, vol. 2 (Fall 1991), pp. 102–14; Thomas Carothers, "The Observers Observed," Journal of Democracy, vol. 8 (July 1997), pp. 17–32; Jørgen Elklit and Palle Svensson, "What Makes Elections Free and Fair?" Journal of Democracy, vol. 8 (July 1997), pp. 32–47. For a reaction see Robert A. Pastor, "Mediating Elections," Journal of Democracy, vol. 9 (January 1998), pp. 154–63.

15. For analysis on this outcome in Ethiopia see Terrence Lyons, "Closing the Transition: The May 1995 Elections in Ethiopia," Journal of Modern African Studies, vol. 34 (March 1996), pp. 121–42.

Index

Carter, Jimmy, 25, 28, 42, 56
Carter Center, 48, 53, 55, 56
Catholic Church, 35
Civil society: demilitarization of politics, 13–14, 15–16; efforts to create, 62–63, 68–69; need to create institutions, 6, 13, 16
Civil wars. *See* Liberian civil war; War termination
Cohen, Herman J., 25, 29
Conflict management: roles of elections, 4–5. *See also* Peace agreements; War termination
Congress, Liberian. *See* Elections, Liberian (July *1997*); House of Representatives; Senate
Constitution: Liberian, 46
COPAZ (National Commission for the Consolidation of Peace; El Salvador), 10
Côte d'Ivoire, 29, 90n.5; refugee camps, 47, 92n.25; support of Taylor, 26, 30; troops in ECOMOG, 40, 41. *See also* Yamoussoukro accords
Cotonou Accord, 11, 30–32, 36, 75
Council of State, Liberian, 33, 34, 39, 44, 48, 50, 53
CRC-NPFL. *See* National Patriotic Front of Liberia-Central Revolutionary Council
Crocker, Chester, 82n.8

Dayton Accords, 17, 67
Defense Areas Agreement, 20
Demobilization of militias, 11–12, 13–14, 42–43
Democratic Republic of Congo, 5
Democratization: civil institutions needed, 13, 16; as goal of postconflict elections, 2, 62-63, 67; slow pace, 68
Disarmament: of Liberian factions, 42–43. *See also* Demobilization
Displaced persons. *See* Refugees
Doe, Jackson, 21, 26
Doe, Samuel: death, 24, 84n.23; election (*1985*), 21, 26, 55, 82n.8; military government, 21–22, 37, 45; nostalgia for rule of, 37; overthrow

of government, 20, 22, 23, 83n.14; political party, 44
Dokie, Sam, 33, 65, 95n.7

ECOMOG (Economic Community of West African States Cease-Fire Monitoring Group), 72–73; alliances with Liberian factions, 29, 37; casualties, 38; control of economic assets, 26-27; cooperation with UNOMIL, 31–32; costs, 38; criticism of, 29, 40, 90n.6; deployment throughout Liberia, 41–42; disarmament process, 42–43; disengagement as goal of elections, 18, 19, 39, 42; establishment, 23; expansion of forces, 27, 31, 40, 41; failures, 29, 37, 38; fighting with factions, 24, 26–29, 30, 32, 33, 35, 36; implementation of Abuja Accords, 34–35, 41–42; intervention in Liberia, 20; intervention in Sierra Leone, 65; involvement in trade, 30; peace-enforcement mission, 24, 31; purpose, 23; restructuring of Liberian army, 65–66; roles in election, 54, 55, 56, 93n.50; security during campaign and election, 51, 52, 56; Tanzanian and Ugandan troops in, 31, 32; Taylor's opposition, 23-24, 25, 84n.21; United Nations support, 19, 31-32; U.S. and European support, 24, 41, 90n.11; Yamoussoukro agreements, 26
Economic Community of West African States (ECOWAS): Committee of Nine, 39, 50; efforts to implement Liberian peace agreements, 28, 65; goals in Liberian peace process, 19; intervention in Liberian civil war, 23–24, 84n.18; Liberian election certification, 54, 56; Liberian election preparations, 46, 47, 48–50, 54; members, 82n.1; peace talks sponsored by, 24, 25, 39–40; sanctions on NPFL, 29, 30; Standing Mediation committee, 23; tensions within, 26, 29, 30, 40. *See also* ECOMOG